HOW TO TAME A
WILD
B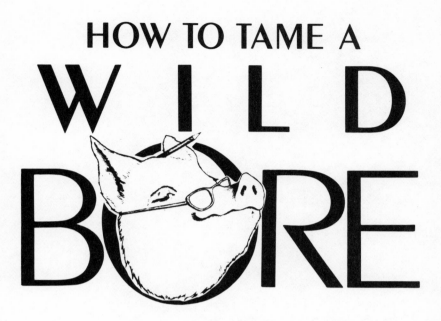RE

& OTHER
FACTS of LIFE
WITH
LEWIS

THE SEMI-TRUE CONFESSIONS OF THE THIRD
MRS. GRIZZARD

Kathy Grizzard Schmook

Peachtree Publishers, Ltd.

Published by
PEACHTREE PUBLISHERS, LTD.
494 Armour Circle, N.E.
Atlanta, Georgia 30324

Manufactured in the United States of America

1st printing

Library of Congress Catalog Number 86-61542

ISBN 0-931948-99-1

To the beautiful state of Montana — a haven,
a heaven, and home to all that I treasure.

HOW TO TAME A

WILD

BORE

Introduction

Before I married Lewis Grizzard, I thought it was rather unusual that the media would play up the unfortunate fact that he had been married and divorced twice. In later years, and now that I, too, have become a Grizzard statistic, I am simply amazed at the interest in his marital upheavals. I have been questioned in private, interviewed by major newspapers and magazines, and besieged at cocktail parties by men and women all asking the same question: "What was it like being married to a 'good old boy' like Grizzard?"

Well, I'm tired of polite, evasive answers. Good breeding can take you only so far. It has finally occurred to me that I could be doing Lewis' readers a great disservice by not sharing "the rest of the story" with them. After all, he makes quite a ballyhoo over his three marriages and divorces. I hear it on radio and television, on tapes and records, read it in the newspapers and on bumper stickers, ad nauseam. So now I feel as though a certain amount of retaliation is in order . . . just to set the record straight, you know.

In *How To Tame a Wild Bore*, I will speak not only of my experiences involving life with the "Cyrano of the South," but at times I will give a bit of additional insight into the Billy Bob Baileys of the world. I come highly qualified for this job, having been a charter member of the AMA (Accrue More Alimony) Foundation. I also have a close personal relationship with Dr. Ruth; I won first prize in a contest sponsored by Gentlemen's Quarterly for guessing the number of socks used in the Jim Palmer Jockey underwear ads; and I once was solely responsible for the mating of a Canada goose with a duckbill platypus due to training I received from the head quack of Ducks Unlimited.

I will also attempt to answer some of the questions I have been asked, such as:

— "Did you and Lewis fight?" If you enjoyed reading about Armageddon, you're going to love this.

— "Was Lewis romantic?" Only the manager of the S&H Green Stamp Redemption Center near our house knows the depth of his romanticism.

— "Do men like him show affection and can they ever be tamed?" Only Gunther Gebel Williams knows for sure.

I am here as the most recent (last I heard, anyway) ex-Mrs. Grizzard to dispel the myth of "poor Lewis . . . he's been married sooooo many times." Hey! What about me? I'm the one who marched down the aisle that Sunday with visions of "The Donna Reed Show" and "Father Knows Best" running through my head. I'm also the one who began to wonder several months after the "I do's" if they weren't looking a little too far south for Josef Mengele.

So, here it is . . . in print, the compelling story that answers the question of what happens when a "good old boy" goes bad.

A kiss from Dad after the walk down the aisle

First Time Ever I Saw Your Neck

Only the very stout of heart could survive an evening with my dad. He was a very funny man to those of us who were used to his irreverent humor but a nightmare to those who weren't. The dinner table was his favorite arena, and his favorite occasion was when we had some unsuspecting guest over to eat.

"Bet you could eat corn through a picket fence with those teeth," he'd taunt our friends who had the misfortune of not being able to hide their braces.

Or to anyone who may have had an oversized pimple in a strategic area, he'd say, "I didn't realize you were an actress. Are you trying out for the Cyclops part in the new Sinbad the Sailor sequel?" If they didn't have acne when they got to the table, they sure had a good case of it when they left.

My mother played the straight man for him, although she tried desperately to quell Dad's language and his antics. But my sisters and I encouraged his depravity. And we learned quickly to pay attention to every quip and twang of sarcasm that came our way, because we knew that sooner or later it would come back like the backspin off Jimmy Connors' racquet and hit us in the face.

All this taught me to have a sharp eye, a quick wit, and a warped mind . . . essentials in appreciating good humor. So when I met Lewis Grizzard, it was quite natural for an attraction to form between us.

I remember mentioning to my mother that a friend had arranged a date for me with Lewis. Mom gushed about how she loved reading his sports column because he had "such a cute sense of humor."

"He'd better," I said. "There's sure nothing funny about sports." Frankly, if I couldn't find it in the society section or on the front of the *Enquirer* as I checked out at the grocery store, I figured it wasn't worth reading.

But Lewis and I did meet, and despite my friend's warning — "Of course, he's no one you'd ever get serious over. He *has* been married twice, you know" — I eventually made it thrice.

How did it happen? When did it all begin? It began on a crisp fall afternoon with a blind date to a Georgia Tech football game. And somehow I think a necklace had a lot to do with it.

I was taking out the last of my electric rollers and checking the results of the previous night's wrinkle-removing cream when I heard the knock on the front door. I yelled to my precocious five-year-old daughter, Lisa, to answer it. I listened carefully through my bedroom door for the sound of his voice and her reaction, since I knew it would be an honest one.

"Hi," he said with all the warmth of the Incredible Hulk. This was met with total silence while my miniature Joyce Brothers summed him up.

Then to my horror, I heard her ask, "Are you a girl?"

"I don't think so," the voice replied. "Why do you ask?"

"Because you're wearing a necklace, and only girls wear jewelry," she said matter-of-factly.

At that point I went for the window, trying to make a quick getaway, but was caught by my baby sitter, who had arrived a few minutes earlier. She dragged me back in and threatened to call my mother if I didn't behave. I pleaded, telling her I was sure my date was a stiff wearing an unbuttoned shirt, a well-positioned chest toupee, and gold jewelry from every appendage. Liberace I could not stomach on my first blind date in twelve years.

My case collapsed, however, when my daughter walked into my room and announced loudly, "Hurry up, Mom. Your weird date is here, and he won't talk."

I followed her into the living room to greet this Grizzard fellow and was pleasantly surprised to find he was not a transvestite. However, my eyes were instantly drawn to the gold chain at his neck . . . or I should say, the *green* chain. Apparently he had not sunk a lot of money into it, because the chain formed a green ring around his throat.

All the way to the game he apologized for his necklace, "which seemed to upset that darling kid of yours," and he said he hoped it didn't bother me.

"Personally, I prefer my men unadorned," I said, "especially when their jewels begin rotting on their bodies."

That comment led us into a discussion on the whys and wherefores of men who "chain up." I shared with Lewis my theory that a lot of men feel compelled to experiment with "bodily baubles" as they pass through transitional stages of their lives, such as divorce, an affair, or a religious experience. Others do so just to make a statement about their financial status.

He confessed that he had raced out to the drugstore and purchased his chain immediately after his last divorce because all his single friends were wearing them.

Then he asked, "Do you think it's too big?"

"Is *what* too big?"

"My necklace," he said.

"Oh, that. Well, I don't want to hurt your feelings, but it sorta makes me sick," I confessed. "It's not real gold, it's turning green, and it's too . . . sturdy. Let me put it this way: It would make a great bicycle chain."

Our date to the football game was pleasant enough. I suspect we both spent a lot of time being thankful that the other wasn't a "double bagger"

The Cloister . . . with slacks instead of jeans

(a date so ugly that you have to put a bag over your head as well as theirs). In fact, I was rather enjoying myself . . . until the wind picked up and Lewis' nose began to run.

The amazing thing is that it never quit running the rest of the afternoon. And naturally he wasn't carrying a handkerchief. He finally excused himself at half time, and I gladly accompanied him to the restroom area where I presumed he would excavate the problem.

I waited outside for what seemed like hours before he finally exited. His nose was clean, but now his zipper was down. Not only that, but there was a wad of toilet paper stuck on the bottom of his shoe that trailed all the way back to his abandoned stall. I didn't feel that I knew Lewis well enough to come between him and his toilet paper train nor to mention the zipper. So I hemmed and hawed for several awkward moments, hoping that sooner or later he would look down or feel a draft.

Luckily a radio announcer who knew him walked by and yanked on the tail of his shirt, which was peeking out of his fly. Lewis spun around on his heel, which twisted the toilet paper up around his ankle, and fled back into the men's room.

RAGS WON'T GET YOU RICHES

That first date told me beyond a doubt that Lewis was lost when it came to sartorial matters. It's not that he was a slob; he just didn't spend much time in front of mirrors. And that's one of the things that attracted me to him, because I've never liked vain men. He was completely unaffected, and his humor was spontaneous. And he dressed the same way — unaffectedly and spontaneously.

As Lewis and I spent more time together, he began to lay out the blueprint of his future for me: He would continue to write a column for the newspaper before eventually becoming syndicated, write humorous books that would appear on the *New York Times* best-seller list, and finally he'd build to a crescendo with an appearance on the Johnny Carson Show.

I was impressed with his goals and ambition and told him so. But I also gently explained that the Porter Wagoner look was out, and that if he was going to make it big, he needed to take more interest in the way he dressed. I explained to him in great detail about the "dress for success" philosophy and how clothes can "make the man." I told him that clothes can tell a story or sing a song about a person, and so far the only thing I was hearing when I looked at him was "Turkey in the Straw."

We talked about accessories, and I told him these should never be overlooked. For instance, I said, a little thing like shoes can make a tremendous difference in a person's overall appearance. As we were discussing shoes, I noticed that Lewis had on his *only* pair, his Bass Weejuns. The heels were so worn down that they looked like a pair of slip-in mules, so I suggested that he might consider having them resoled.

"What's that?" he asked.

I knew right away that I had my work cut out for me.

Soon after our discussion on shoes and the pros and cons of their proper care, Lewis was called to New York on business, and I accompanied him. On a Saturday afternoon as we strolled up Fifth Avenue, he began to limp.

"What's the matter?" I said.

"I've got something in the bottom of my shoe," he said, stooping to take a look.

"I'm bleeding!" he yelled. "What if I get blood poisoning? I could die!"

From embarrassment, I presumed. I found an empty pack of matches in my purse and placed it over the nail shining through the insole of Lewis' shoe. Then I led him down the street to the Gucci store, home of some of the finest leather goods made.

We looked around for a few minutes before I asked a salesman if he could show us some shoes. In one of his stage whispers that could break glass, Lewis announced, "I don't trust no grown man with his hair slicked down and parted in the middle, and he is not puttin' them dancin' slippers on me!"

He refused to try on the shoes, so I had to guess his size while megaphone mouth continued to expound. "Kitty, this proves you don't know what you're doin' in here. This is nothin' but a gay department store created to rip off a bunch of snooty Yankees."

I managed to purchase a pair of shoes in spite of Lewis, and they even fit. I did not realize at the time, however, that I had created a monster. Since that day, he has seldom been out of his Guccis.

ROPED AND HOGTIED

The more I was around Lewis, the more I became aware of his argumentative nature. He would argue with anyone about anything, if it rubbed him the wrong way, but nothing set him off quicker than dress codes. This became embarrassingly clear to me at a very swank resort in Florida.

Lewis had been asked to give a speech at a convention in a lovely old hotel on the east coast of Florida, and again I had accompanied him. We arrived early and went to the dining room to see what time the banquet started before his speech. Suddenly we were accosted by an indignant maitre d', who told us that Lewis could not enter because he didn't have on a tie. I ran for cover.

As the fight ensued, Lewis began yelling, "Look, I'm the star here! I can wear anything I want to. You are a mere employee!"

To which the Frenchman with the Bronx accent replied, "I don't care if you are the President of the United States. You are not going to set foot in this dining room without a tie!"

Unfortunately, Jimmy Carter was the President at that time, and Lewis had met him. So he went to the lobby to call his friend Jimmy. I intercepted him on the way and convinced him that the President was probably vacationing in Libya with Billy, and that maybe we should go to the room and let him cool off a bit. It was obvious to me that the "garçon" wouldn't have allowed Nehru into his dining room without a tie.

We went to our room, which was a little efficiency with a kitchenette, and unpacked our clothes and a few groceries we had brought along. Lewis continued to rave about the "uppity waiter," but suddenly I saw a smile come across his face. Remembering the bacon we had brought for breakfast, he went to the refrigerator and took out a slice. He wrapped it in a piece of plastic wrap and used a piece of thread from my travelling sewing kit to tie it around his neck.

I stared in utter disbelief as we headed back down to the dining room with his "tie" displayed proudly around his neck. When we walked in, the maitre d' raced over to inspect us, and at the same moment the president of the organization Lewis was addressing arrived to take us to our seats. As he took my arm and led me to the head table, I glanced over my shoulder and heard Lewis, in a barely audible voice, snort "Oink, oink!" in the maitre d's ear. Then he continued on to the seat of honor, leaving a porcine perfume in his wake.

A few years later we were travelling in Europe and spent a few days in Florence, Italy. As part of our shopping, we decided to visit the Gucci store (since

Lewis was addicted) and compare shoe prices to those in America.

The salespeople spoke a little English, so I asked a very attractive salesman to help me. As I was following him around asking questions and trying to understand the answers, I suddenly heard, "Yeehi! Giddyup!" Then I felt a stinging on my rump. I turned in shock to see Lewis L'Amour holding a riding crop, getting ready to mount up and swat me again.

"Hey, Kitty, they've got some pretty kinky stuff in here," he said, and I knew then that the "Frascati factor" (irrational behavior is directly proportional to the amount of wine consumed at lunch) had gone into effect.

I continued to try and converse with the salesman and to lose Lewis in the process, but to no avail. He was following me around, still holding the crop and using his leather lingo while he sang little ditties like, "Let's Gucci on Down," "Put on Your High-Heeled Guccis," and, his favorite, "Take Your Guccis Off the Table, Mabel, and Give the Cheese a Chance to Stink."

At that point I knew it was hopeless to ignore him any further, so I took him over to a rack of silk ascots and asked if he knew what they were. Being a man about town, he replied, "Certainly I know what those are. They're sissy handkerchiefs in the shape of tongues." Then he cleverly held one up to his mouth as he stuck out his tongue.

"No, Lewis, that's not exactly correct," I said, trying to maintain a modicum of respect. "These are actually a form of neckwear chosen by more astute dressers. In fact, you would look very nice in one."

As he stared at me in stunned silence, I continued. "These are primarily used by the Italians in the spring as a mating aid. They are in fact a type of aphrodisiac that increases the sexual drive in women to such a degree that they find it impossible to keep their hands off any man found wearing one."

He was fondling an ascot by then, and I knew I had his full attention. "Do you have to wear it over a regular tie?" he asked.

When I assured him that no other tie was required, he bit. Right then, in Florence, Italy, Lewis Grizzard bought three ascots which he wore throughout the rest of our trip in Europe.

You read it here first.

A LETTER IN HIS MAILBOX

One of Lewis' trademarks, in addition to his Guccis, was bluejeans. He wore them everywhere he went long before the style was generally accepted. As long as they were clean, unripped, and fairly unwrinkled, I never complained too much . . . except for the time he tried to wear them at the Cloister Hotel on Sea Island, Georgia.

The Cloister is an old resort in a lush setting on the Georgia coast. It is a bastion of elegance and ocean front charm, a haven for honeymooners, discerning vacationers, and the favorite choice of major corporations for a convention site. In all the years I have visited Sea Island and stayed at the Cloister, I have been aware of one policy that never changed: Saturday night in the dining room and clubroom was always formal, although black tie was optional.

Lewis had been asked to speak at a meeting in the afternoon, and after his speech he went back to the room to rest. As it got close to dinner time, we took showers and began to dress for an evening of dining and dancing. I finished dressing first and went onto the balcony to wait until he was ready to go. Finally he said, "OK, let's do it."

I went back inside and gasped. "What have you got on?" There stood Lewis in an ultra-suede jacket, a shirt unbuttoned down to the center of his chest, and a pair of dirty, wrinkled bluejeans.

"What's wrong with this? I've got on my Guccis," he said.

"Lewis, this place is so formal on Saturday nights that you *could* wear a tuxedo!"

"Why? Who died?" he said with a smirk that deserved a smack.

"Just because someone dresses for dinner in a tux doesn't mean that there has been a death. Now, you put on a tie and find some dress pants, or we can't go in the hotel to eat. And then there *will* be a death, 'cause I'm starving!"

He finally gave in, reluctantly, and changed into dress slacks. When we were greeted by the maitre d' in the dining room, Lewis couldn't resist saying, "Two for the wake. Did anybody bring fried chicken?"

One interesting thing about jeans is that they are capable of making a nonverbal statement about the wearer. They can actually send messages according to their cut, fit, and color. For instance, a saggy butt usually denotes a happily married man; a stiff bright blue with any sort of exposed stitching will be worn by the computer-minded sort who has just gotten the word on leisure suits being out, or by anyone connected with the PTL Club; jeans with flared legs and that have shrunk to "clam digger" length are reserved for grandfathers (who are excused), older conservative politicians, science teachers, and tour leaders.

Faded tight jeans, on the other hand, are always a sure sign of trouble. When my friends used to ask, "How can I tell if my man is cheatin' on me?" the first thing I'd ask is "How's he wearin' his jeans these days? Got a letter in his mailbox? Can you look at him from the front and count the fruit in his bowl?"

If they answered yes to either of these questions, I felt it was my duty to inform them that it was just a matter of time before they would hear one of the following from their man: "I just need a little space," or, "I need some time to get it together," or, my favorite, "I'm trying to get my head screwed on straight."

These are actually eviction notices in code that men send to their wives and girlfriends, meaning that their tight jeans have finally caught the eye of "Cricket" at their favorite bar and disco, and they'll soon be moving on.

Lewis looked very good in jeans, but we were constantly arguing over the fit. He insisted on buying them too tight, and he would squeeze into them till his stomach doubled over while he zipped and tried to button them.

"How can you eat with pants that tight?" I would ask.

"Kitty, if I wore them any looser I'd look like a librarian. Besides, these are better for my image. You know how you women are — always looking at men's butts."

"Yeah, right," I said. "Most of the women who look at your butt are looking for a place to kick it."

COMING OUT OF THE CLOSET

Lewis didn't have a full-length mirror in his apartment when I met him, so he couldn't see what he looked like from the waist down. It's probably best that he couldn't, since some of his jeans defied description; they had holes in strategic places, stains on the knees, and some even had notes for his column written on the front of the legs. When I complained, he said he had several new pairs but could never find them.

One day when I was over at his place, we decided to do some spring cleaning, and he asked me if I would help him clean out his closets. I agreed on the condition that I could throw away his old, worn-out clothes.

I had spent several years in the retail business, and for a while I had done executive shopping for businessmen. Most of these men travelled a great deal and didn't have time to shop for themselves. At times they would ask me to rearrange their closets and then buy whatever I thought they needed to update their wardrobes. I thought I was fairly proficient in this field, but when I took a look at Lewis' closets, I was shocked. Ramar of the Jungle would have had a hard time fighting his way through them.

The first closet we attacked was supposed to be a linen closet, but Lewis had turned it into a Jockey cemetery. It was knee-deep in dirty underwear.

As I pulled on my L. L. Bean Maine hiking boots to wade through the disgusting display of dirty derrière wear, I asked Lewis, "What in heaven's name happened in there?"

"Well, I'm not real sure what to do with underwear after I've worn it for a few weeks," he said.

Apparently his last wife had left before she could finish his course in Laundry 202. She had only gotten as far as teaching him how to buy the underwear and how to put it on . . . not wash it. So when it got dirty, he threw it in his closet. And when it ran out, he just went to K-Mart and restocked.

"But, Lewis, why are you saving the old ones?" I asked in disbelief. "Are you collecting them for a scrapbook? Do they each have a sentimental meaning attached to them? What happens when your closet gets full?"

Without blinking an eye, he said, "I'll just move."

I followed him down the hallway and into his main closet, a rather large walk-in. At least, I *tried* to follow him in. We had to climb over his inflatable kayak, which had become semi-inflated when Lewis was experimenting with his new pump. He didn't want to let the air out because he couldn't figure out how to fold the boat back into the small bag it had come in. He was just going to wait until the next time he went camping and then take his boat out . . . in about eight more months.

He had fishing poles hanging from the ceiling with all the lines tangled, baseball caps, a collection of beer bottles from around the world, a poster of Roy Rogers and Dale Evans on one wall and a poster of Francis the Talking Mule on the other. There seemed to be no organization to the clutter, so we had to start from scratch.

Most men arrange their closets in order of priorities by putting the things they wear most often near the front. Then they put all their pants, shirts, and jackets together. As I looked at the things in Lewis' closet, I could tell that he had not grasped this concept. And I was having trouble implementing my plan because I honestly could not identify most of the things in his closet.

The first thing I discovered was about twenty pairs of knit pants with elastic waists that Babar the Elephant could have worn. The label in one pair said, "Atlanta Tent and Awning Company." Lewis explained that at one time in his life he had ballooned up to 222 pounds, and he just didn't have the heart to throw away these reminders of "the good old days."

Next I found several pairs of short, brightly colored polyester pants that Jethro Bodine would have been proud of. Lewis said he had ordered them from the Glow Worm Hiking and Canoe Outlet Store in Glimmer, Tennessee; if you bought one pair, you got five more free. The label said they were made of chenille and nylon.

I commented on the brilliant britches, and Lewis said, "Those pants are very valuable because you can wear them to a party or use them to fish in. They're indestructible."

What they were was indescribable. I figured the only thing they could have been good for was trying to attract rainbow trout.

I explained to Lewis that he should never light a match near his closet, because the synthetic fumes from the resulting flash fire would kill him for sure.

In Lewis' defense, I suspect his bad taste in clothing was the result of his recent move back to Atlanta from Chicago. He was probably suffering from "synthetic syndrome." That's a rebellious state that transplanted rednecks go through when they return South from places like Antarctica or Chicago. Those afflicted with the syndrome wear as much nylon and rayon as possible in order to make up for all the time they spent wearing mukluks, fur-lined parkas, and long-handled underwear.

Interspersed between Lewis' synthetic pants was quite an array of shirts. Most of them were T-shirts he had won in beer drinking contests or tennis tournaments benefiting Marvin Mitchelson. In addition to those, he had synthetic shirts in a kaleidoscope of colors. Some looked like Picasso had created them, while others appeared to have pictures from Sea World on them — lots of otters, porpoises, mermaids, and parrots.

He had only two jackets, which were crammed in the back of the closet. One was the perfunctory college madras, and the other was a navy blue polyester with lots of little "picks" all over it. The pocket was ripped off on one side, and I asked Lewis why he had not had it fixed.

"Every time I wear that damn coat, which I try not to do very often, I get to my front door and hear the phone ringing inside. I hurry and unlock the door, run into the kitchen, and I always get yanked back by a pull-thing on the front of one of the drawers. It rips my pocket every time."

"Do you want me to try and fix it for you?" I asked.

"No," he said, "it wouldn't do any good. It'd just keep gettin' ripped."

We finally finished wading through Lewis' indoor landfill, and as I began to make my recommendations, I spotted a hanger hidden by the infamous blue jacket. On it were four neckties. As I described earlier, Lewis was not into ties, but he said he kept these around for emergencies, "like in case I have to go to church sometime or I get invited to lunch at some snooty country club on a Sunday afternoon." No danger there, I thought.

The ties were sherbet-colored and looked as if they had been tie-dyed. Painted on the bright colors was some sort of intriguing design. As I looked closer, I noticed that the design was in fact little words — dirty little words, as in profanity — written upside-down and sideways. I was appalled, but Lewis said you had to be lying down or standing on your head to read them, so it was all right to wear the ties out in public.

When I asked why he kept such vulgar ties, he said they had a great deal of sentimental value to him because one of his neighbors in Chicago, Raoul, had designed them. "He called them his 'high ties,'" Lewis explained.

I couldn't resist asking why.

"Because his inspiration came from getting high on funny cigarettes. They finally locked him up for selling inspiration around the neighborhood. I guess that makes these ties a limited edition, huh?"

We can only hope so.

When it appeared that we had uncovered everything in the closet, we began throwing out the things Lewis couldn't (shouldn't!) use. That didn't leave much, but what was left confused him.

"You've thrown away my favorite things, so now I don't know what to wear with what," he complained.

I remembered the little tags called Granimals that used to be popular in kids' clothes to help them know what went together. For instance, they had doggies, kitties, ponies, duckies, chickies, and bunnies. As long as the kids matched ponies with ponies and so forth, they'd never get their stripes and plaids confused.

So I went through a couple of magazines and traced jungle animals for Lewis. I colored them, cut them out, and attached them to his clothes so he could match up animals in the mornings. He had lions, tigers, gorillas, hyenas, elephants, and even some camels. I made a chart showing that lions and tigers could go together, but woe be unto anyone who tried to pair a camel with a gorilla. He finally got the hang of it, and after several months of trial and error, he was able to remove the zoo from his closet.

ARE THOSE BOOTS LOADED, PARDNER?

Although Lewis' taste in clothes occasionally left me cross-eyed, I am thankful that he never got into the urban cowboy thing. Oh, he toyed with it once by buying a pair of boots — Dingos, the choice of city slickers — but even that didn't last long. The first time he wore them, he stepped on a tube of Preparation H that had fallen on the bathroom floor, and the ointment left a stain on the toe of one of his boots. He swore that the stained boot had shrunk, so he never wore them again.

I suggested that if he wouldn't wear them, maybe he could just sit on them and "kill two boots with one butt."

I suspect the real reason Lewis never went in for the cowboy fad was that we witnessed too many of them showing their hindquarters in public. They'd swagger into the local disco or bar trying for all the world to look like Clint Eastwood but looking instead like Deputy Dawg.

The first tip-off was their boots, which usually were made of naugahyde instead of leather and showed not the first sign of manure on the outside (that was all on the inside). And then there were those hats! Some with jewelry, some with feathers, and once I even saw one with sea shells (probably left his sea horse tied up outside).

Lewis and I witnessed a donnybrook over a cowboy hat one night in a bar in Fernandina Beach, Florida. We were sitting at a table when in walked a Waylon Jennings lookalike in his finest "outlaw" get-up. He had on a large black hat over shaggy hair and long, thick sideburns, and he was dragging on an unfiltered Camel. We all knew that his name was Shane, because it was carved on the back of his leather belt.

Shane sidled up to the bartender and ordered a "B and B — that's bourbon and branch," and then slowly turned to peruse the patrons. He left no stone unturned when it came to the ladies, although I couldn't help noticing that he never missed a chance to catch a quick glimpse of himself in the mirror behind the bar.

Suddenly he could stand it no longer. A pretty young barmaid came up next to him to place a drink order, and he leaned over and whispered something to her. At first she tried to ignore him, but after he did it again, the exasperated waitress finally said, "No, I don't want to ride your pony!"

Just then the bartender, who unfortunately for the waterfront wrangler was the barmaid's new husband, raced around to the front of the bar and caught Shane tough, right on top of the left ear. Shane hit the floor like a cow pie, but on the way down his hat caught on the edge of the bar, and off it came . . . it, his sideburns, and the rest of his "rug."

It seemed that Shane was none other than Hopalong Hairpiece, and the evidence lined the Stetson beside his face on the floor. He recovered quickly, however, and before you could say "Wildroot Creme Oil Charlie," he was gone, leaving a full B and B on the bar.

Lewis paid a good deal less attention to the barmaid for the rest of the evening.

Wine, Women, And Pork Bellies

As someone who has been on the dating scene more times than I care to admit, I am forever hearing the lament from my friends that there aren't any available men around. "The ones with class are all married, and the really cute ones are all gay," they complain.

Maybe so, but I contend that the *real* reason there aren't enough men around is the "I can't be alone" syndrome, which is more prevalent than Ralph Lauren's polo stick. Allow me to explain. Most men are so insecure that they must have a woman around constantly. She may serve as an emotional crying towel, a parrot that only knows the word "stud," a cook like mama, or maybe even "mama" herself.

Whatever the role, these men need a woman close by. They're terrified at the thought of spending the night alone or, worse yet, risking rejection in their attempts to pick up a fresh one somewhere along the way. So you can be sure that nine out of ten times when such a man says "So long" to his woman, he's already got the second string lined up and ready to kick off. He never sits out a quarter. And that's why you never see them "loose" on the streets.

Women, on the other hand, are used to being alone and/or rejected. We were raised on it. For example, throughout our teen-age years we had to sit ladylike and wait for dates to call us; we were at the mercy of the boys. The world's greatest pencil-necked, pimple-faced geek could call at the last minute for the Junior-Senior prom, and we would jump at the chance to go simply because he was a date.

But if no one called, we had to sit home, eat Mallo-Mars by the hundreds, and listen to our mothers tell us how pretty we were and that "the little boys just don't know it yet." Nice try, Mom.

Later we experienced the same ignominy with blind dates — sitting around waiting for the call. But these calls came with a catch.

You'll seldom find a man who will simply pick up the phone on a friend's recommendation and ask a nice young lady to dinner. No, first he must interview the prospective client over a drink after work, or, if he's a bit more daring, he may even pop for lunch. Either way, he figures he hasn't invested more than an hour and a few bucks.

If he has been stung in the past by a blind date who resembled Mr. Ed, he may insist on a drive-in movie where he can inspect the merchandise in dark and in private. If she passes there, he may ask her out for a daylight date.

But *never* would he consider starting with a legitimate dinner date unless he has seen a life-sized nude photo of the potential date and has received ahead of time a financial statement from her broker. He wouldn't take a chance on being seen with a woman who is too old (anyone who cannot remember what flavor Lip Smacker she was wearing the night she was crowned Homecoming Queen in high school), too fat (anything over a size six), or — God forbid — wearing late-in-life braces on her teeth.

Never mind if "the other woman" is a leaf brain and giggles at the thought of all those cute donkeys in New York City when someone mentions the boroughs. If she *looks* good, she gets the date every time. The rest of us wait by the phone wondering why *Flashdance* has taken the place of the wedding march.

When I remember some of the blind dates I have been stuck with, it burns me to think that most men won't take the same chance. I used to enjoy the challenge and excitement, as evidenced by the fact that I went out with Lewis Grizzard, sight unseen.

I am relatively tall, and once a friend fixed me up with a date so short he was able to adjust his bow tie by looking at his reflection in my gold belt buckle. What made it even worse was that I had worn a new pair of spike heels that made me five inches taller than usual. It wasn't so bad when I was sitting, but when we'd get up and walk, I was forced by good breeding to practice the "duck strut," where you bend your knees but keep the upper torso erect. This makes you closer to the height of your date . . . and very sore the next day.

My munchkin date loved to dance, so after our evening of dining and a concert, we headed to the local disco to dance the night away. At least, he did. I waddled around the floor like Daffy Duck, all the while aware of my towering size and my aching back.

We had many drinks before he finally took me home, which improved his spirits if not mine. As I hobbled up the steps to my front door, "Shorty" told me something that burned into my memory: "I never mind going out with tall women," he said, "because when we're nose to nose, my toes are in it, and when we're toes to toes, my nose is in it."

I never squatted for a little guy again.

Another time I had a blind date so bad that my housekeeper answered the door and said I didn't live there. The man persisted, so she reluctantly let him in. Then she raced upstairs and told me I had a headache.

"Are you crazy?" I said. "I feel fine." "Well, you're gonna wish you had an aneurysm when you see your date," she replied.

All of the etiquette my mother had taught me came into play when I first gazed on this man. He was wearing a black sleeveless T-shirt, baggy blue-jeans, wing-tip shoes, and a chain around his waist.

Minutes before the "explosion" at the White House

To complete this somewhat tough look, he had a leather bracelet with silver spikes on one wrist and a contradictory looking Spiedel Twist-o-Flex on the other. I was speechless.

He took me to his apartment, where he fixed a dinner comprised totally of Lean Cuisine frozen food. "I'm on this diet, you know, and it's the only thing I'm allowed to eat. Want some more Fish Florentine? Less than three hundred calories."

Those were the last words he spoke to me. He was so shy he simply could not make conversation. There were a lot of motorcycle magazines on his coffee table, so I assumed that was his thing, but I could never draw him into any sort of discussion.

Now, in such situations, I feel it is my responsibility to carry the load (good breeding, again). And if need be, I can talk the ears off a chicken. But as I continued to chat away about fascinating topics such as my highly intelligent children, the great sale they were having on Erno Laszlo cosmetics at Neiman's, and the always stimulating question of metric conversion, painful blisters began to develop on the inside of my mouth from sheer overuse.

Fortunately my eagle eyes spotted the new phone book at just that moment, so I asked my date if he had ever wondered what the last name in the phone book was. He shook his head no, and that was the only opening I needed.

For the next two hours we scanned the directory for weird names with unusual spellings, or, more exciting yet, we looked up our friends and family. Finally it was ten o'clock, and I told him I simply had to go because I was having an operation the next morning at six, and consequently I needed a lot of sleep and couldn't eat or drink anything else that night.

He was suspicious and asked what kind of operation I was having. Men get very squeamish when you mention anything about female anatomy, so I very demurely looked away and said, "I have to have something removed that's growing on my you-know-what." I was in the car and on the way home faster than Cinderella trying to beat the clock. I also escaped that embarrassing moment of declining the good-night kiss, because he obviously wasn't interested. He'd rather have sucked the exhaust pipe of a big Harley than risk getting near my diseased "thing."

AT&T HAS BETTER LINES

Lewis never liked blind dates (they could see right through him), but he also didn't like being alone (a victim of the "I can't be alone" syndrome). So before we were married, he spent a good deal of time trying to acquire company.

One night we were in the same bar but not together. He was with some of his drinking buddies, and I was with some friends after work. I was able to witness firsthand how he operated, and I quickly understood why women treated him like a case of herpes.

He strolled up to his first victim and said, "Grizzard's the name, news is my game."

The woman flipped him a quarter and said, "Call somebody who gives a damn, Scoop." Then she walked off.

A couple of things happened at that point. First of all, the bartender who had overheard the rebuff buried his head in the ice machine to keep from howling; and secondly, all of Lewis' cohorts who had also heard the unforgettable reply were gurgling in their beers and spraying each other. Lewis, the chagrined lothario, had no choice but to amble over to his audience and say, "She was a dog up close. Couldn't even drink her to a five."

He was persistent if nothing else, though. Instead of giving up, he just changed lines.

"Hey, sugar lips, wanna see my tattoo?" he said to the next target. He stood in front of her like he was delivering the Gettysburg Address, but when he got no reaction, he leaned down on the bar and sort of wrapped himself around her like a lizard. While in this intimate position, he whispered to her, "Most times it says, 'Shorty's,' but sometimes it says, 'Shorty's Truck Stop, Chattanooga, Tennessee, 243-6599, Call About Our Sunday Smorgasbord.'" Then he gave her a teasing wink and stood back as if waiting for her blouse to unbutton itself.

But little did he know that a snake would grow hips first.

"I don't do Braille," the woman said, "and it's obvious that only a blind woman would go out with you."

The guys at the table nearly drowned.

His latest line, I hear through the grapevine, is, "'Scuse me. I'm Lewis Grizzard. Have we ever been married?" I also hear that it works about as well as the others.

Lewis seldom tried such lines on me, but in many ways he was equally inept. For example, on our second date, I went over to his apartment to cook some steaks for dinner. He volunteered to do all the kitchen work while I relaxed and enjoyed myself in front of a romantic fire. I could hear him in the kitchen as he puttered around, and before long he appeared with a jug of red wine.

"Did you bring a corkscrew?" I asked.

"It won't do if it don't unscrew," he quipped, obviously pleased with his selection, Red Thunder port.

We set up his backgammon board and played for quite a while before I asked if I should check on the steaks. "Sure," he said, so I got up and went into the kitchen. I couldn't find any meat frying on the stove or broiling in the oven, so I called him in.

"They're right here," he said, proudly pulling out the pot and pan storage drawer under the oven. There they were, all right — stone cold. Lewis mumbled something about his broiler being broken, so we put the steaks in the refrigerator and went out to dinner.

On another far more historical date, we were in Washington, D.C., where we were meeting a friend who was on Jimmy Carter's staff. He had invited us for an informal tour of the White House, after which we would go to lunch.

Following a brief security check, we were greeted by our friend, who took us through some of the briefing rooms, the Oval Office, and the rose garden. In the middle of the tour, Lewis asked our host if there was a restroom he could use. We waited outside while Lewis took care of business.

And did he ever. It sounded like the Iran-Iraq war was being fought inside that bathroom. After about fifteen minutes of muffled explosions, our host asked if Lewis was ill.

"No more than usual," I said. "Last night we got in late, after the hotel restaurant had closed, so Lewis had the bellman bring up a pint of Haagen-

Dazs ice cream. But there was no spoon with it, so rather than wait for the man to bring one up, he ate all the ice cream with a ball point pen. This morning he swore that gave him gas, so I guess that's the problem now."

At lunch, when Lewis reached for his fork, our friend offered him a ball point pen instead. Lewis didn't laugh.

A STAR IS BORN

After we had been seeing each other for about a year, an interesting thing happened to raise Lewis' stock in the dating game. He left the sports department and began to write a humor column for the newspaper, and suddenly he was the "daily darling" of Atlanta. Almost overnight he was a star. He was asked to make speeches, do radio and TV talk shows, give magazine interviews, and his caricature was even found on billboards. Now he had a new problem with women — they were falling all over him.

Unfortunately for Lewis, that's precisely when we decided to get married.

Married. What is it about that word that doesn't mix with Lewis Grizzard? Seems like every time it is said around him, a hex is immediately placed on his bride-to-be.

I guess I should have been suspicious when he was late for our wedding because a book autographing party ran long. Or I certainly should have had doubts that night when he invited his accountant and his best friend Jerry over to our Peachtree Street hotel (which was selected because it was near another autographing the next day).

"Lewis, would you please explain to me why you had to ask your friends over *tonight*, of all nights, to watch the basketball game with you?" I asked in utter frustration.

"I always watch the Georgia games with my friends," he said as if it were so obvious that it didn't need saying.

"And you couldn't miss just one game so that we could have an uninterrupted honeymoon?"

"Why should I do that? Besides, Jerry would get mad."

"Oh, *he* would get mad? What about *me*?" I asked indignantly.

"You're supposed to get mad . . . that's what wives do."

By the end of this heated discussion, I was so infuriated that I took off my wedding band and dramatically placed it on the dresser in our bedroom. In an equally dramatic gesture, Lewis took off his shiny new band, too, and threw it across the room at me.

Seeing his rage build, I decided to be conciliatory and put my ring back on. Lewis agreed to do the same thing in an attempt to save our eight-hour-old marriage, but he couldn't find his ring. It was lost in the shag carpet. Finally the next morning, while he was gone to his autographing, I combed the rug with my fingers until I found it. But by then I knew it was going to be a rough row to hoe.

Of course, the women who were chasing the new media darling didn't make it any easier. I naively assumed that once we were married they would cool off a bit. Wrong. Some of them had no shame. They would proposition him at speeches, while we were dining out, and even when we were shopping. I soon learned how to end these advances quickly, however. I would wait until they were rambling through their pocketbooks in search of something for him to autograph and to write their phone numbers on, and then I'd appear out of nowhere with a pair of size forty-two BVDs and say, "Here, honey, these should fit. And try not to have any more of those nasties in them, OK?"

Nowhere was safe, and these women didn't care if he was with his wife or not. Who did they think I was, Eleanor Roosevelt? They'd scratch his head, pat his fanny, kiss his cheek, and some would do a basic rub on him the way a cat in heat does, tail up and all.

One of the most horrific realizations I had to come to was that women not only made passes at Lewis in person but through the mail as well. I made this discovery when I visited his office one day and was waiting at his desk for him to finish a column. Larry Flynt could have filled six good issues of *Hustler* with the memorabilia that some of Lewis' female admirers sent him. There were ladies' undergarments, lewd pictures of his "fans" in female wrestling garb, baked goods sent by women assuming that the fool he was married to couldn't cook, and all kinds of homemade crafts.

My personal favorite of these was a sort of voodoo doll that was supposed to resemble Lewis with a huge "love arrow" going through the heart. When I asked him what it meant, he said this woman was a witch and wanted to "charm" him into being all hers. I told him the only thing she was going to charm was Clarabell, because that stupid doll looked just like Howdy Doody.

But it was the letters that really made me mad. My mother always told me not to be forward with boys; according to his fan mail, these women wanted to be forward, backward, upside-down, sideways, inside out, and then some.

For example: "I know how much you loooove biscuits, you cute thing, and I know you never get any homemade ones, so if you'll call me, my friend Twanta and I will come over any Saturday night. We'll wear our string bikinis and practice our football cheers for you while the dough rises." Or: "Lewis, you are the sexiest, most sensual man I have ever seen. Let me come over and scratch that big thick head of hair [thick head was right]." And then there was just the blatant, "I've got it. If you want it, come and get it."

SPAM, BAM, THANK YOU MA'AM

Of all the mail Lewis got, the remarks about his wife's cooking were the ones that infuriated me most. It was obvious they didn't know who they were dealing with. My Aunt Viola Lynn (we called her "Aunt Violin"), taught me at an early age that the way to a man's heart was through his stomach. (At a later age I learned there was an alternate route.) She taught me that fried chicken to some men is what Fay Wray was to King Kong.

I remember being in a business school once right out of college, and they were trying to teach me to type, take shorthand, and work business machines. A hopeless case, I admit. I came home dejected one night after cheating on a shorthand test and still failing it. Aunt Violin was over visiting my mother, and as she put her arms around me, she gave the worst advice anyone ever did: "Honey, don't worry about that silly school. Southern girls don't need to know how to do anything 'cept have babies and cook reeeeal good."

That night I left business school and entered Aunt Violin's school of collard greens, mashed potatoes, crisp fried chicken and okra, pole beans, and fruit cobblers that could make a grown man cry. Then we moved on to her Italian favorites. We made fresh pasta with spinach and tomato noodles, sauces with fresh herbs she had grown, and gorgeous green salads.

She taught me how to cook the way the French do by carefully selecting the most sumptuous vegetables and not overcooking them but delicately preserving their natural flavors. We made choron, béarnaise, béchamel, and champignon sauces, and when mine would curdle, as they usually did, she'd give them to her cat and make me start over.

Her Chinese dishes were incomparable. She took me to the Chinese grocery store and taught me about the special vegetables they sold and how to cut them just right so they would cook properly in the wok. This was my favorite lesson, because Aunt Violin was totally deaf in one ear, and I could sing all my cute wok songs in it while we cooked. There was "Wok of Ages, Cleft for Me," "Whistle While You Wok," "Jailhouse Wok," and I always finished up by asking her what her favorite "Wok" Hudson movie was. She always said the same thing — "Sweetie, you have such a pretty singin' voice, and yes, you'll have a husband one day." Boy, was that an understatement, even if she didn't hear me right.

I graduated from Aunt Violin's school of culinary delights with "frying" colors, and I enjoyed cooking for my friends in the years following. And then I met Lewis.

I had looked forward to the day we were married and I could begin to cook for him. He was sure to be thrilled. I assumed he would savor everything I fixed, but that was not the case.

He loved Southern cooking, which was fine, but that was *all* he would eat. He would on occasion eat a steak, but they tended to hurt his teeth, so he stuck to country fried steak. Over and over again.

And bread. I'm so sick of hearing about Lewis' passion for homemade biscuits that I could scream. The truth is that what he really prefers is white loaf bread. The kind that goes directly to the top of the mouth and becomes glue-like, then fuses to the top of the tongue until it eventually melts away.

I would get teary-eyed remembering the hours Aunt Violin and I practiced brioche . . . only to have Lewis come into the kitchen and holler for light bread and country fried steak. Finally one day he said, "Kitty, if you'd stop trying to cook like Julia Child and start cooking more like Aunt Jemima, I'd be a lot happier." Unfortunately, Aunt Jemima was one of the few women who didn't write him a letter offering to cook for him.

If the truth be known (and that's what I'm here for), Lewis' favorite meal was really . . . Spam and pinto beans. That's correct — he would beg for fried Spam with a tad of onion sautéed in a skillet and then covered with those polka-dotted beans.

"I don't know how to cook anything that looks like Mighty Dog," I said one evening out of frustration.

"My first wife used to cook it for me all the time," he replied smugly.

"When one marries at fourteen, what can one expect? Perhaps you would like to dine on some of the poke salit growing out by the dog's pen."

We would then compromise and I would fix pork chops and lima beans, but in the years following our divorce I had nightmares about canned luncheon meat. In those awful dreams Lewis would strap me in a grocery cart and sing and dance his way through the store, pushing me along the whole way . . . "Spam in the morning, Spam in the evening, Spam at supper time; be my little pork belly and

love me all the time," he would chortle as he stuffed
can after can in the cart, winking to let me know the
hour of preparation was growing near.

HUNKERIN' DOWN BY CANDLELIGHT

I suppose Lewis' female letter-writing fans
thought they were appealing to his romantic nature,
but I've got bad news for them — he was about as
romantic as artificial insemination. That was part of
our problem. I was the hopeless romantic, and he
was the prophet of doom. Nevertheless, I held on to
the hope that some romance would rub off on him.

On our first anniversary, we went out to a club
that had live music. I asked one of the members of
the band to play "our song," which at the time was,
"You Light Up My Life." The man smiled and nodded, but little did I know that my beloved spouse
had beaten me to the punch. Lewis shuffled up
behind me and yelled to the band, "Hit it!" They
instantly broke into a lively round of, "Hunker
Down, Hairy Dogs," while pretzel legs performed a
maniacal version of the Mashed Potato, all the while
yelling above the music that he had won the state
dance contest in ninth grade doing that same step.
Most impressive.

And gifts . . . I was always dreaming of the day a
man would read my mind and present me with the
kind of gifts I saw in magazines — a Bulgari gem or
maybe an around-the-world cruise on the QE II. No
such luck with Lewis.

Once, in a fit of romantic depression, I even forgot one of the lessons Aunt Violin had taught me: Never, under any circumstances, have a serious fight with your man before *any* holiday, such as your birthday, Christmas, Valentine's day, Mother's Day, and in extreme cases Ground Hog Day. It was the day before my birthday, and Lewis and I got into a tremendous fight. We made up the next night, but it was too late for him to do any shopping and he was caught without a gift.

In a valiant attempt to still the troubled waters, he called the twenty-four-hour drugstore, desperately looking for some Faberge Cologne in a locket ("Tigress-scented," I heard him specify). The druggist told him he had not carried that item since bouffant hairdos were in style, so instead he suggested some hair spray with glitter in it or some Almond Roca candy.

Lewis hung up the phone and disappeared into the basement. When he came back upstairs and joined me in the den, he handed me a birthday gift straight from his heart — an enchanting picture of Heisman Trophy-winner Herschel Walker wearing only his silver britches and holding the Georgia mascot, "Uga," who was wearing no britches and was slobbering all over himself.

A hopeless romantic? No, just hopeless.

THIS MUST BE A BAD CONNECTION

I suppose the biggest problem that Lewis and I had in our marriage was a failure to communicate.

He understood nothing about the way women think, and I had no idea why he loved his typewriter more than me, since it couldn't even cook. So to avoid as much confrontation as possible (which wasn't very much), we often talked in code.

At first neither of us knew exactly what the other meant by various little comments. But after awhile, we began to decipher each other's cryptic lingo. When we figured out what was *really* being said, trouble started.

Following are some typical examples of GSP (Grizzard Sensory Perception) messages:

KATHY: "I know it *looks* like real diamonds, honey, but it only cost thirty dollars. These zirconiums are amazing!"

Translation: Tiffany's let me pay thirty dollars down and thirty dollars a week for the next two years.

LEWIS: "You know I'd like to take you to the Masters in Augusta if I could. But I've got to work the whole time, and only a bunch of guys are going anyway. No wives. And there aren't any extra tickets. I'll only be gone three weeks."

Translation: Lewis didn't have a ticket either but was tagging along with his newspaper pals. He'd sit in a nearby bar and drink till they were finished working. Then they'd all head over to Hilton Head Island for tennis, fishing, and chasing.

KATHY: "I promise I'm not mad that you didn't come home last night. And if you insist that you slept in the garage under your car, then I believe you."

Translation: I hate your guts, you dirty liar, and I'm going to fry your eggs in grease I scraped off the garage floor.

LEWIS: "You know I love it when your mother and father and sisters come over for dinner . . . especially when your mother reads the Bible after dinner."

Translation: I will develop an ulcerated colon before I stick around for another family visit.

KATHY: "Oh sure, love, it's fine with me if you have your tennis team over for a cookout on our anniversary."

Translation: But it'll cost you a thousand dollars after I have it catered and buy a new dress to cheer myself up.

LEWIS: "Hey, kids will be kids. I know potty training is tough on the little guy. I'm just glad I realized it wasn't a Tootsie Roll before I sat on it."

Translation: If that little brat gets near my car again, I'll flush his disposable pants down the toilet while he's still wearing them.

KATHY: "Really, I don't mind if you take your sweet new literary agent Giselle out to dinner to discuss business. The doctor said I should be over the flu in about a week."

Translation: And when I am, I'll maim the lousy scuz bag.

LEWIS: "No kidding, I love cats. They're so . . . mysterious. This nice tiger-striped one you gave me is just what I wanted. Look, he's rubbing against me already."

Translation: I hate cats! And this one is going to be rubbing against the inside of the dog's jaws as soon as the "gift horse" turns her back.

KATHY: "Are you sure you want another vodka tonic, darling?"

Translation: If you lean over the table any more you'll need a snorkel to keep from drowning in your gazpacho. And the table of ministers next to us is nodding approval because they think you're speaking in tongues.

LEWIS: "No, really, your hair looks good short."

Translation: Maybe it'll grow out soon, Butch.

KATHY: "Of course I don't think it's too extravagant for you to spend five hundred dollars for a new graphite tennis racquet."

Translation: But the next time you fail to show up for dinner, I'm going to use it as a colander.

LEWIS: "I swear, your fanny does *not* look big in those pants. I can't tell that you've gained a pound, sweetheart."

Translation: Or should I say, "sweathog"? My God! You went to sit down on that bar stool and I thought the Hindenburg had landed.

KATHY: "I promise, Lewis, it's a great column. It's really cute."

Translation: If they run that piece of nonsense, I'm applying for the job next week.

LEWIS: "I think it's wonderful that you and your friend Trudy can get away for a week and take the kids to the beach."
Translation: There is a God, after all.

A new ring guard at Christmas brought a smile

Manicure by International Harvester

Personal hygiene and grooming habits are unique indicators of a man's self-image, but strangely enough we often overlook them. Women notice right away if a man is tall or short, fat or slim, bald, wearing glasses, or knows how to smile. Based on these quick observations, we may classify men under "Wow," "Passable," "In a Pinch," or "Goat." But we never consider whether the man in question bathes on a regular basis, gets haircuts and shaves frequently, or even brushes his teeth daily. We just take for granted that he does.

Where Lewis Grizzard was concerned, I learned that no one should make such assumptions. Some of the things that most men do as second nature never entered his mind. Take tooth care, for example.

Lewis complained about his teeth from the first time I ever met him. He seemed to have a never-ending toothache, but he could always rationalize why he was in pain. Maybe he had been excavating his mouth with a paper clip and had stabbed himself in the gum, or in an emergency he had tried to unscrew the non-twist top on a beer bottle with his teeth and was suffering from the cracked aftermath. It never occurred to him that there might be an odious omen in his discomfort.

It was my assumption, inane as it now seems, that most men would visit a dentist at sometime in their adult life . . . especially if they had cavities in their front teeth that showed every time they smiled. I offered to make appointments for Lewis on several occasions, but he always had a variety of excuses for why he couldn't go.

I know he was conscious of it, because one morning before he had to give a speech to a large and influential group of local businessmen, I caught him trying to use "White-Out" on a particularly dark and cavernous spot. His efforts failed, however, because he couldn't keep his mouth open long enough without drooling for the liquid cover-up to dry.

He often used his peep-hole cavity for entertainment purposes. For example, he discovered that he could emit a rather melodious whistle through it. One night I heard him do a rousing rendition of "Dueling Banjos" with his friend John "Plucky" Ben Suggs playing his guitar and Lewis playing his cavity.

That's Lewis letting the good times roll . . .

. . . and later in another role, that of stepfather

On another evening at his favorite Italian restaurant, I saw him consume almost an entire plate of spaghetti with pesto sauce without ever opening his mouth. He sucked the pasta through the hole between his front teeth, and he would have been able to finish off the whole plateful if he hadn't encountered a pine nut in the sauce.

His favorite trick, however, was to try and impress my children by blowing enormous bubbles with a mouthful of "Big League Chew" through his blowhole. They would watch attentively as he chewed and blew, chewed and blew, knowing full well that sooner or later one large bubble would explode on his face. They were right. And when it happened, Lewis would invariably end up with bubble gum covering his mustache. Now, this was *real* entertainment for a couple of kids who enjoyed hearing a grown-up use every four-letter word they had dreamed of, because that's just what Lewis did. Especially when I would suggest that he'd probably have to shave his mustache to get all the pink out of it.

Recently Lewis' murderous molars caused him a real problem, one far more serious than a sticky mustache. An infection from one of those cavities attacked his replaced heart value and necessitated a second heart surgery. I hate to say it, but . . . On second thought, I wrote a short poem which says it best. I've entitled the poem, "Don't Give Me No Wooden Nickels, George, I'll Just Take the Teeth."

How many times did I say,
"Will you go to the dentist today?
Your teeth are rotting, that's for sure.
I see each month you have fewer and fewer."

But you waited till the pain did come,
Then were left with nothing but gum.
This proves my theory — By being a chicken,
They had to "stomp on that sucker" to keep it tickin'.

So here in this book, after all your woe,
I cannot help but say it just once "mo":
Lewis, you coward, I told you so!

HAS THE CLOD BEEN SHOD?

Nails, both the finger and toe varieties, are another area of personal hygiene that men frequently overlook. They bite 'em, tear 'em, or just ignore 'em until they're good for only one thing. (Do they pick only at red lights, or all up and down the road?)

Men in the movies always seem to have manicured hands. Their nails are closely clipped and clean with a marvelous hint of sheen to them. These are the hands that women long to have wrap a silk shawl around their shoulders, or slip a surprise diamond on an unsuspecting finger, or maybe even open the door of a penthouse suite in Paris overlooking the Champs Élysées for a weekend getaway.

But alas, most of us never see these men in real life. We have to settle for the biters, pickers, probers, and household mechanics.

Take accountants, for example. They use their index fingers as pacifiers for the first four months of the year. They chew the ends until there's nothing left but a bloody pulp, because these are their line-pointing and adding machine digits. My tax returns always have little drops of blood all over them where my accountant bit his nails into the quick trying to decide if I was filing single or jointly that particular year.

Then there are the men who let food and dirt accumulate under their nails. I once knew a man who was lost in the wilderness for two weeks and managed to survive on the nutrients stored under his fingernails.

And toenails . . . Why don't men clip them? Lewis would let his grow until they began to curl under his feet like runners on a sled. Then he would crawl into bed and thrash about all night, leaving me with severed arteries below the knees. I finally had to resort to wearing "Protecto Hose," designed to save legs and ruin a marriage.

But the real danger occurred when he would finally decide to cut those things. Anytime I entered a room and heard the clipping noise, I would retreat to the garage for the lid to the garbage can, which I'd use as a gladiator's shield when I went back inside. There would be Lewis sitting on the edge of the bed, naked, using a tool that looked like a combination oyster shucker and horseshoer. Toenails would be flying everywhere.

These missiles had real force behind them, and they would lodge in the drapes, in the carpet like punji sticks, and once he even landed one in the overhead light fixture — such a lovely sight to lie in bed and gaze at in the evenings.

HAIR TODAY, GONE TOMORROW

Some of the most difficult decisions men face in their lives deal with their hair. They worry about it twice as much as women and change it more often than their underwear.

They deal with traumatic questions such as, "Is now the time to add those ash blond streaks, since Shaundra and I have finally gotten it together?" Or, "Shall I take these fourteen hairs on the left side of my head and sweep them allllll over to the right side and just forget about a part?" Or, "How would I look in a perm? Women like curly hair, but I'm not sure it would look natural." (I've seen freshly permed men whose heads looked like something Meadowlark Lemon would dribble.)

And then there's the most frightening of all quandaries — hair today and gone tomorrow. *Bald*. The very mention of the word sends men running for charlatans and looking for frog's teeth under full moons. The same people who promise women a more robust bust in thirty days delight in selling men creams, salves, and hair-growing hormones. (What would happen if they got the bust cream and the hair cream mixed up? Would women be combing their bosoms and men be wearing bras on their heads?)

As soon as "chrome dome" gets the old hag and the kids ensconced in their new double-wide trailer, which he graciously provided for them after the divorce, he's off to see the rug merchant. And before you can say "a little dab'll do you," he's off to the bars to test his new mane.

He may get away with it for a while, but sooner or later his new little coquette will discover the bare facts: "Honey, why isn't your pretty black hair blowing in the gale-force winds that just swept our sea-side love-nest into the ocean?" Or, when he absent-mindedly leaves the top down on his new Porsche at the One Minute Carwash, and Bambi says, "Oh, pumpkin, that's so cute the way your hair doesn't even get wet. Water just rolls off it like nothing happened." Right. Nothing happened except his new "weave" looks like someone painted it on with a Magic Marker.

Lewis' problem with hair was just the opposite — he had so much he didn't know what to do with it. When we first met, he used a blow dryer, which produced the "fluffed" look. Then after we were married, he decided that every minute he wasted drying his hair was a minute that could have been spent serving up another one at the tennis courts, so he adopted the "wet" look with water dripping down the back of his Izod.

Then one day he was cited in a magazine article as having one of the worst hairstyles in Atlanta, so he dedicated himself to improving his look. He tried it long, but he said that made him look like a liberal, which was tantamount to being a leper in his circles. Then he tried it short, but he said that made him look gay and that he'd rather be a leper. I suggested that he wear it medium-length and part it down the middle — quite the intellectual look, I thought. But when he did so, he bore an amazing resemblance to Alfred E. Neuman.

It was the freckles, we believe, that made Lewis look like he'd just stepped off the cover of *Mad*. And he hated them. He felt they undermined his authority and gave him the appearance of a young whippersnapper who had never gotten his comeuppance in life. He once overheard a man at the newspaper telling a joke, and the punch line was, "freckle puncher." Due to his intense paranoia, Lewis immediately presumed the joke was about him, so that night he poured glue over the keys of the man's typewriter.

I hate to admit this, but in his zeal to become an unblemished example of pure Nordic stock, as he claimed to be, Lewis actually resorted to quackery. He ordered through the mail from a Dr. Hugo Whackleman a product called Blendo, which was guaranteed to get rid of freckles or double your money back.

When the tube of Blendo arrived and Lewis read the directions to me, I was perplexed to hear that the ointment was supposed to be used in the sun. Sure enough, Lewis had a speech that weekend on Hilton Head Island, so he packed his clothes and Blendo and headed off to restore "the natural beauty" of his skin.

The results were, at best, tragic. When he walked in the door Sunday evening, I didn't know whether to run and kiss him or stand still and whinny for him. His freckles had sort of all run together — "blended," so to speak — leaving him looking like a pinto pony. True to the advertising, Blendo had left him with fewer freckles, but those left behind were considerably larger than before.

Luckily for Dr. Whackleman, "Old Paint" shed his sunburned skin and returned to his normal, freckled self. But he was utterly disconsolate over the whole affair. To save his self-esteem, I finally found a copy of *The History of the Norsemen*, which proved beyond a shadow of a doubt that Eric the Red, bravest Viking of them all, was in fact red-headed. And everybody knows what goes hand-in-hand with red hair.

ARE THOSE GLASSES HALF FULL OR HALF EMPTY?

A becoming pair of eyeglasses can be most attractive, but most men would rather squint their way through life than face up to the fact that they're just a step away from a Braille reader.

Eventually, at the urging of a mother or a wife (the subject is *never*, under any circumstances, discussed with a girlfriend because it's so dull), a blind man will break down and go to an optometrist. Once glasses are prescribed, he is faced with another of those perplexing decisions — What kind of frames should I get?

Like the way they wear their jeans, men's eyeglass frames can tell you a lot about them. For example, the tortoise shell or horn-rimmed frame denotes a rather studious, methodical sophisticate. Such men are pictured in *New Woman* and *Cosmo* with a thick book in one hand and lingerie from Frederick's in the other. Sitting at their feet is some pouting, scantily clad damsel in distress begging for the return of her peek-a-boo bra. Men look at these pictures, and visions of Clark Kent go through their heads. Such frames, however, must *not* be round, or heterosexuality is immediately called into question.

Wire-rimmed glasses are usually worn by the more outgoing guy, and he occasionally will tint the lenses so that he can keep an aura of mystery about himself. Such men are usually athletic and have switched over from plastic to wire at the suggestion of their manicurist or hairstylist. In their own coy way, these "cosmetic shrinks" convince their myopic male clientele that Mr. Magoo is not a turn-on and that sporty wire frames might accentuate their sex appeal. Enough said — they're off to capture the aviator look.

Then there's the rebel, the guy who has decided to throw caution to the wind and try out the new colored frames that are available to match every outfit. This sort of man likes to hop over tennis nets and into convertibles without opening the door, and usually drapes his sweater around his shoulders like a fur as he orders another Frangelico at his favorite bar, "The Uppity Yup."

But the man I really feel sorry for is the one who finally decides that *no* style of frames is going to improve his looks. He's tried them all, and when nothing worked, he bought a complete Nautilus fitness machine and even had the hair removed from the mole on his forehead. Finally, in desperation, he resorts to aqua-tinted contacts.

The scenario is always the same. First he struggles for an hour trying to get them in, spilling solution all over his shirt and pants and leaving his eyes bloodshot and watering. Then, squint-eyed and bushy-tailed, he heads for his favorite smoke-filled bar to test his new contacts on some unsuspecting young lady. He saunters up to the first prospect, full of new-found confidence, and says, "Hey, babe, how does a nude beach in Martinique sound?"

Unfortunately, the line loses much of its punch when delivered by a guy blinking more rapidly than an iguana in a sandstorm, so the lady answers, "What's wrong? Did Winkin' and Nod already have dates?"

Lewis' eyesight was so bad that he was utterly helpless without his glasses. And since he was famous for losing them, he was constantly buying new ones. Every time he purchased a new pair, he would experiment with new frames, and with each new look came a new personality.

When we met he was wearing traditional horn rims, and since he was a sportswriter at the time, they combined nicely with his rah-rah talk and saddle oxfords to create a collegiate-looking package.

After we were married, he switched to light-colored tortoise shell rims and immediately became the intellectual humorist, constantly quoting Willie Morris, Roy Blount, Jr., and Art Buchwald. His mood around the house was generally benevolent, and he enjoyed getting into heated debates with me about whether I thought God was a woman and, if so, did She have a beard.

The wire rims that he tried next made him appear more avant-garde, he said, and brought out the social side of him. These he wore for speeches, when we went out to dinner, or when he was on the prowl. The problem with them, however, was that they were so lightweight that after a few too many beers, they would slip unnoticed off his head and invariably be sat on or stepped on. Soon they were all bent out of shape, so Lewis tried to reshape them himself. The result was that the nosepiece always looked like a beak and the legs opened up like a pulley bone to embrace his square head.

Having given up on wire rims, he next went *au naturel* with clear rectangular frames. These were the ones I dubbed his "Dr. Jekyll and Mr. Grizzard" glasses.

The first day he wore them home, I noticed and said, "Oh, did you get some new glasses?"

"Yeah, I broke my wire ones playing tennis this morning, so I had to go to 'This Is a Frame-Up' and pick up this emergency pair," he said.

"Isn't that where Trixie Breasthammer works?" I asked with considerable interest. "The woman you did the column on last month?"

"As a matter of fact, Perry Mason, it is. And the name is *Chest*hammer. She's still struggling to support herself and her four kids," he answered offhandedly.

"Oh, is she still dancing at the Clatterbox Lounge?"

"Sure. That's the only way she can make ends meet, and she is barely making it."

"I don't know about that. Her bare end seems to be 'making it' just fine!" I knew I was on thin ice, but I couldn't help myself.

"Look, just because Trixie does interpretive dancing at the Clatterbox doesn't mean she isn't a wonderful optometrist's assistant. She's the one who suggested these clear frames, in fact. She said she had seen a picture of Prince Charles wearing a pair just like them."

"Are you sure she didn't say Charles Nelson Reilly, 'cause you're the spittin' image of him right now."

"Kitty," he said dramatically, "your humor escapes me. You're just pissed off because another woman chose my frames. I do believe I detect the green-eyed monster."

"If you're speaking of yourself, you look more like a *bug*-eyed monster. Your eyes are so magnified in those glasses they seem to go all the way across your face!"

From that tempestuous beginning, those glasses were always trouble. The minute he would walk in the door wearing them, he would start yelling about something and I'd head for cover.

After about three weeks of escalating warfare, the new "Bugmo" glasses were accidentally left beside Barney the basset hound's food dish. I watched helplessly while in the blink of an eye he chomped down and carried them away to his graveyard for family memorabilia. They joined his collection of socks and underwear, Barbie and Ken dolls, Stars Wars men, tennis and golf balls, bedroom slippers, and satin Christmas tree ornaments.

I should have expected it, but somehow Lewis' next move caught me completely off guard. He tried contact lenses. I didn't think he had the patience for them, and I *knew* I didn't the patience for his trying to wear them. I figured the first time wind blew dirt in his eye we'd have to call in an emergency rescue team. But after one of his pubescent female fans told him at an autograph party, "You have such pretty eyes, you shouldn't hide them behind glasses," Mr. Venus in Bluejeans floated over to see the optometrist and Trixie for his new contacts.

That night I accompanied him as he made an impressive entrance into his favorite hangout *sans* spectacles. He had his usual excessive number of vodka tonics with "just a splash of tonic," his favorite, and fished for compliments on his new look. Before long, however, he was fishing for something else.

As a thick tongue turned his "splash" into "slash," he began making eyes at every female in the bar. When he gave a particularly enthusiastic wink to some redhead, however, his right contact popped out and landed in his drink.

Luckily he spotted it, stuck the tip of his finger in the drink, and reeled it in. Then, on the advice of some veteran contact wearer draped over the bar nearby, he put it in his mouth to "clean" it. But, alas, in his jovial state, he started to talk before taking it back out, and down the hatch the little bugger went without so much as a choke.

Lewis naturally presumed he would be dead in a matter of minutes, but I assured him that this, too, would pass. With his winker out of action, however, he was ready to go home. For the good of the marriage, I resisted making any comment about his contact "missing in eye-ction" and took him home.

I was awakened the next morning by Lewis screaming, "Help me, help me! I'm blind in one eye! Somebody must have thrown acid in it last night." No, just vodka, I told him. But that wasn't the problem. He had forgotten to take out his surviving contact, and it was glued to his eyeball. We finally pried it loose from his bloodshot eye, and before you could say "Mr. Magoo," he was back in glasses.

STAND A LITTLE CLOSER
TO THE SOAP, CHARLIE

Even if a man is able to enhance all of the elements of outward appearance that he deems important — by purchasing a hairpiece woven by Sassoon himself, having his teeth capped until he has a smile like Garfield the Cat, mastering the installation and removal of contact lenses, and even having a little "tuck" done on his jowls — there's still one thing that can destroy the whole picture: body odor.

I realize this may seem like an unpleasant subject, but it's as real as Right Guard.

There are several kinds of perspiration and resulting scents which afflict men. For instance, there is athletic sweat produced by men who exercise a lot and do not put impurities like alcohol and tobacco in their bodies. This is "sweet sweat," because it does not have an offensive odor.

Then there's nervous sweat, which is light enough to be absorbed by a T-shirt but so strong smelling that deodorant won't touch it. One drink after work is plenty with these guys.

And finally there's sweat caused by high temperature and humidity, which is the bane of Southern businessmen. If they're lucky, it'll end with large wet circles under their armpits. But in tight situations — like weddings, job interviews, blind dates, and follow-up visits to the proctologist — it can soak all the way through their coats. By that time, you'll need nose clamps to be around B.O. Bob (they're available at finer drugstores near the earplugs, denture cleaners, and trusses).

Lewis sweated more than any Bahamian bongo player I ever saw. And let me say loud and clear that his was *not* "sweet sweat." (That's why I know exactly where to find nose clamps.)

The first time I watched him play tennis was on a hot summer day. After a couple of games, I got an interesting geography lesson from observing the sweat make its way down his body. Starting from under the left armpit, a shape resembling the state of Alaska emerged. Then came the lower forty-eight and the Atlantic Ocean; these joined with Europe, which had formed under his right armpit. As the temperature climbed on this "dog day" afternoon and the tension mounted in the game, Mexico became visible just above his naval, and it dropped off into South America right at the zipper. Finally, as the match was ending, Antarctica surfaced at the base of his crotch, and Lewis walked off the court looking like a Rand McNally map of the world.

When he came over to give me a kiss, it was all I could do to stifle a "P.U." I offered to walk home and leave the car for him, but he insisted that we go together.

"Then at least leave that shirt here," I said. "It's strong enough to walk home alone."

Before closing this subject, it is worth noting that the term "P.U.," meaning "to stink," is an historic Southern term which came into being during the Civil War. A Mr. P.U. Huckster was a wealthy landowner from Savannah, Georgia, who happened to be in Atlanta during the bonfire Sherman set. Aghast at what he saw and horrified over the news that the Yankees were on their way to the sea via Savannah, he mounted his horse and rode nonstop for a week until he reached his home.

As he arrived at his plantation, soaked with sweat and overcome by nervous exhaustion, his lovely bride, Honey Jasmine, raced to greet him with outstretched arms. But as she got near, she exclaimed,

"P.U.! What the hell have you been rollin' in, darlin'? You smell like a bad batch of chitlins!"

As luck would have it, a Yankee carpetbagger who was a stringer for the *New York Times* and was covering Sherman's march to the sea overheard the remark by Honey Jasmine, misunderstood it, and used it in his story to describe the wretched smell of burning cotton fields. And thus Mr. P.U. Huckster's name has been slandered throughout history, and the entire episode is now referred to as "The Stink Smelt 'Round the World."

Just a little something for you history fans. No extra charge.

Big Toys For Big Little Boys

The dog is often credited with being man's best friend, but I suspect most men would choose their cars over their dogs in a heartbeat. They talk lovingly about their sleek machines using feminine pronouns — as in, "She's a real sweetheart, isn't she?" — and the same men who never remember an anniversary never forget an oil change. (Wives, meanwhile, are discussed in automotive terms, as in, "The old clunker threw a rod and won't be able to mow the grass this week.")

I don't understand their passion for wheels, because I've never cared what kind of car I drive. If it cranks, I say "thanks" and am on my way. For years I drove a Toyota station wagon that looked like it had been retrieved from a Dempsey Dumpster. But it was ready when I was, and I had better things to worry about than cubic inches and crushed velour.

The way a man deals with his cars can also tell you a lot about him. For example, a man who drives a speedy little sports car is either recently divorced or going through male menopause. (Statistics prove that a Porsche is better than Geritol for tired blood, and that a Ferrari can actually raise the testosterone level in men over forty.) It's as if owning a two-seater makes up for all those years of driving family cars, like that '79 Ford station wagon that was a cross between a front-end loader and an ICBM.

Lewis went through this cycle on a regular basis, since he also went through marriage and divorce on a regular basis. When I met him he was driving a little Triumph Spitfire that he cherished. He had just purchased it on his return to Atlanta after three years in Chicago, and he loved to put the top down and drive to work and to the tennis courts.

The only problem was that Lewis is not exactly mechanically inclined, and this car seemed to *always* have something wrong with it. So Lewis would drive the twenty-five miles back to where he had bought it, jerking and sputtering all the way, only to have the service department tell him that he had forgotten to release the hand brake. Another time he called them in a rage to have his car towed in after it had quit. They called an hour later to tell him he was out of gas.

But he loved that car in spite of the problems, because it symbolized his independence and freedom from some "mean old woman," as he so succinctly put it. So I humored him and put up with the embarrassment of arriving at parties with my hair blown and my clothes wrinkled. That is, until one night after dinner at Atlanta's posh Capital City Club.

We had finished a late dinner and were headed home when, about two blocks from the club, the car made a funny noise and stopped. The engine was still running, but the car wouldn't go forward. Surprisingly enough, however, it would go backwards.

I said, "Lewis, why don't you just leave this piece of junk right here, and we can call a cab . . . or even the police."

"That's the stupidest thing I've ever heard," he said. "Don't you know we're in downtown Atlanta? There wouldn't even be an oil spot left on the road tomorrow. Some drunk Yankee would steal this car in a minute!"

"But, Lewis," I argued, "if they can only go backwards, they won't get very far."

"That's what they said about Sherman, too, Kitty, and look where he got."

I ignored this nonsequitur and asked, "So what are we going to do?"

"Why, we're going to back home, of course." And we did — for the full six miles to Lewis' house. I slid down in my seat, hoping that no one would recognize me.

Even Lewis finally lost faith in the little sports car, however. The steering wheel actually came off in his hands one morning as he backed down his steep driveway, and the car ended up in a ravine across the street. Lewis was convinced that his car had been sabotaged, since someone had left a pink flamingo in his yard the night before. But just in case it was an omen instead, he traded in the spiffy roadster.

Being an up-and-coming young columnist/author, he decided it was time to indulge himself in a more sedate automobile, something to reflect his new station in life. So he bought a Cadillac Seville. And how he loved that car. But once again, he was victimized by "sabotage."

Shortly after we were married, Lewis went out of town on business and left the Cadillac at home — with strict warnings that I was not to drive it. The next morning when I went out for the newspaper, however, his car was gone. It obviously had been stolen sometime in the night.

When I finally located him to tell of this heinous crime, he did not ask if the children and I were all right, nor did he ask if the perpetrator had entered the house and stolen anything else. His only comments — after accusing everyone from the leader of the Gay Liberation Movement to Stokely Carmichael to the sports department at the newspaper — were, "Don't tell me they got all my Merle Haggard tapes!" and, "Oh, God, my tennis schedule was on the back seat. Now what am I going to do?"

I told him exactly what he could do and hung up.

The beloved Caddy was recovered several days later, along with the tapes and the tennis schedule. Lewis told the police to be on the lookout for a bum, "because anyone of good breeding would have taken the Merle Haggard tapes."

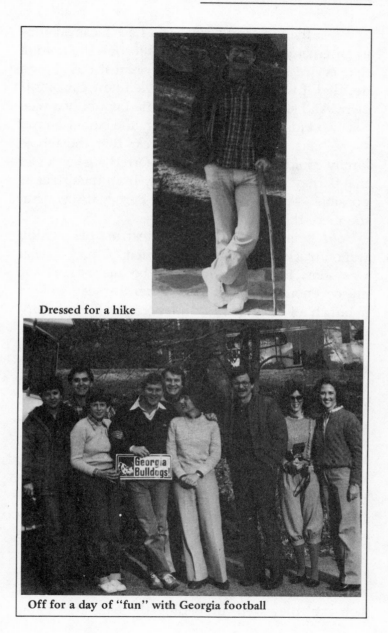

Dressed for a hike

Off for a day of "fun" with Georgia football

When the kids and I borrowed Lewis' car one day in an emergency and afterwards it took the man at the service station two days to clean it out, Lewis decided it was time for us to have a new car of our own. And since he had just married not only a wife but two kids and a dog — Barney the basset hound — he said we needed a large car that the whole family could ride in. He also preferred a *long* car, so that Barney could ride as far away from the driver as possible — the reason being that Barney threw up at the mere thought of a car ride.

So Lewis bought us an indestructible station wagon/truck, which he nicknamed "Chuck." That was short for "Chuckwagon," because there was always enough leftover food under the seats to feed a bunch of wranglers. And because Barney "up-chucked" every time we hauled him anywhere.

Lewis stayed as far away from Chuck as possible and told us to do the same with his Cadillac, but I fondly remember one day when he was forced to take our car. He was supposed to pick up the president of his publishing syndicate at the airport, but when he went out to get in his car, it had a flat tire. It seems that he had run over my son's G.I. Joe fort, which had been carefully constructed out of a garden hoe, a rake, and an axe. It was the rake that got him. There wasn't time to have someone from the service station come and change the tire, so Lewis was forced to take Chuck.

He arrived at the airport just in time, collected his business associate, and headed for a hotel. It was not until they were unloading the bags that panic set in. As the publishing executive leaned over to retrieve his briefcase from the floorboard, Lewis spotted a large grease stain on the bottom of his stylish khaki pants and the tell-tale McDonald's French fry container in the crack of the seat. Then he saw a half-eaten Jolly Rancher embedded in the back of the man's blazer, and a semi-licked green sucker stuck to the bottom of his Guccis.

Lewis never drove my car again.

But true to form, after a couple of years of marriage Lewis got the "bucket seat blues" and traded me, the kids, Barney, and Chuck in on a sportier model. Sure enough, the first place he went after our divorce was the Mercedes-Benz dealer to pick up a sporty 380SL. I certainly understood. After all, no freshly divorced yuppie is complete without one . . . two tops, of course.

One day he came over to deliver an alimony check (which he claimed would dress Nancy Reagan for a year and put him on food stamps) and to show off his new car. We stood around the parking lot of my condominium admiring his expensive toy. When I asked him what all the symbols on the switches meant, he said he didn't know, but he began trying them to see what happened.

First the tape player ate his favorite new Julio Iglesias tape. I was especially pleased by this, since Lewis had just told me his new "single theme song" was, "To All the Girls I've Loved Before." Then the electric convertible top got stuck halfway up. And then lights started flashing all over the dashboard.

"Hand me the owner's manual so I can figure out these damn buttons," he said. But when he opened the book, he discovered that it was written entirely in German.

As he drove away that warm spring day, cursing about some "dirty Nazi car salesman," one of those wonderful spring storms popped up out of nowhere and doused the new Mercedes and its driver. I made sure to laugh loud enough for him to hear me.

IT'S NOT WHETHER YOU WIN OR LOSE, IT'S HOW YOU LOOK

Whether a man's hobby is his car or hunting or golf, there's one thing you can always count on — he'll be outfitted to the hilt. Men spend hours flipping through catalogs and magazines like *Abercrombie & Fitch* and *Field and Stream* trying to convince themselves that camouflaged land rovers, flannel-lined photographer's vests, refrigerated backpacks, computerized running shoes, and stereophonic tennis racquets are as essential as groceries on the table.

My dad is without rival in this area. He cannot enjoy himself unless he feels he is properly equipped in every way. For skiing in Vail, he turns into "Sausage Man," zipped into a skin-tight elastic suit from head to boots. For shuffleboard at The Homestead in Virginia, a cravat and short, black leather gloves are a must. For an unassuming day of canoeing at the lake, he looks like Lloyd Bridges, with wet suit, flippers, tanks, and a spear gun for killer rabbits. And for an afternoon ride on horse-back, he dons a gorgeous plaid hacking jacket and sleek jodhpurs.

Lewis' sporting passion was tennis, and like the other four most important things in his life — beer, county music, work, and Georgia football — he was very intense about it. At times he couldn't even enjoy playing because he was so worried about his backhand, or tennis elbow, or his second serve. And, of course, he had to be properly outfitted with special racquets, balls, glasses, socks, sweat bands, and underwear.

He played year-round — indoors, outdoors, dou-bles and singles. Anytime I would dare complain about how much time he spent at the tennis courts, Lewis would tell me I should be thankful he didn't play golf "because it takes all day." But I never saw the difference. He could make a tennis match last all day and into the evening.

He and his team would play their morning match and then, win or lose, they'd sit under a tree, drink beer, and commiserate for an hour of so. Then they'd spot some unsuspecting newcomer, taunt him by saying he walked like Renee Richards, and before you could say "pop top" the grudge match would be underway. And it would end just after dark back under the drinking tree.

The only thing he really hated about tennis was mixed doubles. He would get paired with women at tournaments who would happily bounce out to greet their "celebrity" partner. But by the end of the match, they would have had more insults hurled their way than a referee at a wrestling match. Lewis was never satisfied until they left the court in tears.

He despised seeing women anywhere near a tennis court, especially when he had to play next to them, and he denigrated their tennis by calling it "serve and chat." The only thing he found interesting about women playing tennis was watching them put balls in their lacy tennis pants and later pull them out to serve. He never could figure out where those balls went "up in there."

But even his passion for tennis paled in comparison to his love of Georgia football. After a couple of red and black seasons with Lewis, I was ready for the University of Georgia to be turned into a finishing school for John Deere dealers with the annual tractor pull as the only athletic event.

The fanaticism began in August as Lewis planned his football schedule. Everything else was secondary. If a friend died during the season, he was horrified that they might schedule the funeral on a football Saturday afternoon.

On game days, he would wake up in a bad mood. I guess it was his way of getting fired up for the game. We would pack our fried chicken picnic, barbecue, coolers of beer, radios, and mini-TVs, and head off for Athens before Coach Vince Dooley was even out of bed. All the way to the game, Lewis would recite to me the life history of every player and coach and then quiz me to make sure I was paying attention.

"Who's the offensive coordinator?" he would ask.

"Whoever planned this trip. I find it *most* offensive," I would answer.

And then he would lecture me about how lucky I was to be an American living in the South so I could have the privilege of watching Georgia football on beautiful fall Saturday afternoons. "That's what this country is all about," he'd say with a straight face.

I developed a retaliatory cheer for such situations: "Two, four, six, eight, let me go regurgitate!"

We would arrive at the stadium by 10 A.M., already worn out from having so much fun. After a four-hour lunch from the back of the car, we'd enter the stadium and sit among people who were so wired they looked like they were doing a live broadcast. How a person can watch a live game, listen to a radio, watch TV, and play it back on a video recorder at the same time is beyond me.

The highlight of my Georgia football experiences with Lewis, however, was the 1982 trip to New Orleans where Georgia played Notre Dame for the national championship. I saw things there that are almost indescribable — female impersonators doing Georgia football cheers and stripping to the strains of "Let the Big Dog Eat"; grown men on all fours biting at legs outside the ladies' restroom; women barking at men in bars.

Being a celebrity Bulldog fan, Lewis was often besieged and asked to autograph programs, shirts, or even skin. One very buxom young woman holding a red souvenir football came up and asked him to sign it. While he was doing so, she pulled up her skirt to show him the bulldog on the back of her underpants. (Her legs reminded me of something from the horror movie *Logula*.) As he handed the ball back to her, I couldn't help seeing the inscription: "To Tami. Thanks for the mammaries, Lewis." Right then I wanted to break into another of my favorite cheers: "Take that ball and shove it! Shove it!"

I really don't understand the zealous, almost violent allegiance men develop for a football team. Lewis has threatened to fight people about the Bulldogs, but shocking as it may be to some people, I remember when he used to love Georgia Tech football almost as much. Don't forget that our first date was to a Tech game. But when Tech fired his friend Pepper Rodgers as head coach, Lewis became a diehard Bulldog fan. At least, that's what he wants everyone to believe.

I think the *real* reason that Lewis decided to hate the Ramblin' Wreck is because the first time I met Tech head coach Bill Curry I commented on how attractive he is. Lewis bristled and said, "We've only been married a couple of months and you're already sniffin' around." After that the only Tech games we saw were when they played Georgia.

Professional baseball games with Lewis could be even worse than college football, because there was no shortage of alcoholic beverages at the baseball games. According to Lewis, a Braves game without beer was like having to stay awake in church without a cigarette.

One of the worst mistakes I ever made was taking the kids — Lisa, eight, and Bruce, six — to a Braves game with Lewis. All the way to the game, Lewis told the kids that he actually had missed his calling in life. He had been drafted right out of high school by the Baltimore Orioles, he said, but his mother would not let him go to camp, so he had decided to write about "the true love of my life" for the newspaper. The children responded by saying, "Wow!" and I with, "Such a waste."

We found our seats, and as usual several of Lewis' fans came over to share their latest joke or to talk baseball trivia. Lewis always introduced me and the kids by saying, "Have you met Moe, Larry, and Curly?"

Sometime during the middle of the game, while Lewis was down on his hands and knees doing his impersonation of a Pentecostal preacher for his adoring fans, a high foul ball headed right toward us. Lewis spotted it and rose for his big play. With the reflexes of a salt-covered snail, he put his hands up and the ball hit right in them . . . and then dribbled down his arms and landed in the lap of an elderly lady sitting in front of us.

The children and I looked at him incredulously. Where was the ex-Oriole draftee? Lewis quickly pointed out that the sun was in his eyes, but I suspected it was Budweiser that obstructed his vision.

The next day he wrote a column describing his heroic catch . . . and how he *gave* the ball to an old lady.

A SUCKER ON THE LINE

Fishing is without a doubt one of the dullest sports I know. Usually the only thing that happens is you end up killing a lot of bait and then lying to cover up your shortcomings. Such is the genesis of fishing stories.

Once I was visiting a friend in Alaska who asked me if I would like to go salmon fishing with him. "No," I demurred, "I'd rather stay here and watch your cat have kittens."

So he went off with a friend and returned late the next day with the most incredible fish I have ever seen. It was a king salmon that weighed just over sixty pounds. I heaped lavish praise on my friend for his catch, and he immodestly said, "Ah, talent surfaces every time."

Finally his buddy stepped forward to admit they had not actually "caught" the fish. In fact, they had run over it with the truck as they were approaching their favorite fishing hole. Seems the salmon had gone aground on a sandbar while trying to swim upstream to spawn, so they had loaded it onto the truck and returned home.

That's about the only way Lewis would have ever caught a fish. He couldn't even get a nibble at Long John Silver's. I think his biggest problem was his temperament; he was just too impatient. If he didn't land a fish within the first five minutes, he would start talking loudly, usually in four-letter words, and the fish would scram.

Once Barney, the basset, made the mistake of going fishing with Lewis. They headed up to the North Georgia mountains, where Lewis wanted to try out the new spinning rod I had given him for his birthday.

They arrived at their favorite fishing hole, and Lewis began practicing his casting while Barney attacked a can of Vienna sausages in the lunch sack. As "Gadabout Grizzard" became more sure of himself, he finally let fly a long one, and instantly he heard a yelp. He had snagged old Barn in one of his droopy ears.

"Jonah," as I referred to Lewis afterwards, had to drive thirty-five miles to the nearest vet to have the hook removed. And it cost him one hundred dollars. And that's no fishing tale.

ANYTHING BEATS FIVE OF YOUR KIND

By far the most abhorrent of Lewis' hobbies was playing cards. Or, to be more accurate, playing poker. It was one of the many ways he rebelled after we were married . . . a way to prove to his single cronies (and to his wife) that he would never be a "wedlocked weenie." So to show that nothing had changed in his life, he invited the gang over once a week for poker.

Waves of nausea sweep over me as I recall those evenings and the odors that emanated from the basement game room. The guys would come directly from the tennis courts, and their sweaty smell would always announce their arrival.

One of them would have been designated as the "caterer" for the evening, and he would have stopped by the local convenience store and picked up a month's supply of Fritos, Doritos, nacho cheese goo, bean dip, assorted luncheon meats, and Twinkies and stale sweet rolls for dessert. And, of course, there were trash cans and coolers full of beer, radios and cassette players, and cartons of cigarettes.

There were never enough ash trays for so many smokers, so they used the floor, paper plates, or what they thought were empty beer cans. By the end of the evening, most of them would have sucked down a pound of ashes by drinking out of cans used as ashtrays.

It was my odious task to direct the clean-up on the mornings after, because "Cool Hand Lew" would still be sleeping (sometimes even in his bed). Besides, he made it quite clear that toxic waste clean-up did not befit a big-time columnist. After trying it myself a couple of times, I determined he was smarter than I thought.

Our Irish housekeeper, Jean, almost quit when I asked her to clean up following one of Lewis' poker parties, but she valiantly gave it a try. After about five minutes, she found me hiding outside and said, "Mrs. Grizzard, I cannot stay down there. Something has apparently died in that room."

I followed her back in and we descended into the chamber of horrors. First my nostrils began to flare. Then my eyes began to water. Finally I was gagging. There were the usual piles of garbage, empty cans and bottles, smoldering cigarettes and cigars, dried piles of bean dip and sour cream, but nothing to account for that awful smell.

Jean appeared on the verge of passing out. "Mrs. Grizzard, I'd rather go back to Belfast and face the terrorists than spend another minute down here," she said. I offered to carry her bags if she'd take me with her.

We were beaten and had no alternative except to call in a specialist — Barney the basset. In he ran and instantly started sniffing like a fiend. He licked the card table clean, finished off some stale potato chips, and then started circling the room and howling. Finally he dived into a corner, licked around, and came out bearing "the smell." When he looked me in the face with watery eyes and breathed, my hair curled.

I thought I recognized the smell as Lewis' tennis shoes without the Odor Eaters, but in fact the source was a baggie filled with an empty sardine can, hard boiled egg shells, and some day-old shrimp dip. One of Lewis' buddies had tossed it in the corner.

I let Barney have another taste and then sent him in to awaken his father with a fragrant kiss.

Bruce defending his gender

Proof that Lewis was a child

Lisa (not Bruce) displaying her ballet form

Clean Living And Dirty Socks Won't Wash

To say that Lewis Grizzard was absent-minded would be like saying Imelda Marcos was fond of shoes. There were two things I could count on every day we were married: the sun would rise, and Lewis would lose at least three pieces of equipment vital to his daily survival. These were his car/house keys, his wallet, and his checkbook.

It never failed. If he was late for an appointment, there were no car keys. If he was coming in from out of town in the middle of the night, no house keys. In the midst of a long checkout line at the grocery store, or at a gas station or an occasional restaurant, no wallet or checkbook — depending on which was the most embarrassing.

Once Lewis was standing in the kitchen with his

car keys in hand and his wallet in his pocket, headed for the tennis court; the next minute he was roaring that someone had "stolen" his keys. I helped him search everywhere, but to no avail. Then purely by chance I opened the dishwasher, and there they were.

"Guess I left them there when I got a glass for some water," he mumbled.

The checkbook would often disappear just as mysteriously. Lewis would put it on his dresser at night, and by the time he was ready to leave for work the next morning it would be gone. Somehow it would have slipped down a crack into his sock drawer, where it would remain until winter when he was forced to wear socks again.

Another time he was convinced that it had been stolen "by some fiend." The only prospective fiends who had been in the house were me, my six- and eight-year-old kids, and Jean the housekeeper, who shivered everytime Lewis even breathed in her direction. He cussed and kicked the whole time he was packing for an out-of-town trip. Finally I told him he had to leave or else he'd miss his flight.

On the way to the airport, we encountered a lot of traffic and at one point he had to slam on the brakes. When he did so, the sun visor flopped down and into Lewis' lap spilled a pack of cigarettes, some B.C. powders, and — wonder of wonders — his checkbook. He then accused the same "fiend" who had stolen it of placing it over the visor just to humiliate him.

One reason he was always losing the checkbook was that he insisted on carrying it in his back pocket, half in and half out. I would warn him time and again that it was going to fall out, but my words fell on deaf ears.

Once before we were leaving for a European trip, Lewis went to purchase our traveler's checks. As always, they told him to keep them in a safe place and to file the receipts separate from the checks in case they were stolen. Lewis, naturally, stuck both in his back pocket.

That evening he came home to change clothes quickly and head out of town for another speech. Running late, of course. He was rushing around the bedroom, barking orders all the while, when I asked if he remembered to pick up the traveler's checks.

"Sure I did. They're in my back pants pocket," he said as he continued throwing clothes around.

I looked quickly but didn't find them, so I gave up for the time being. Later that night I went into his bathroom to get a new razor before taking a bath, and I just happened to glance down at his toilet. There, beached on the sides of the bowl, were our traveler's checks. They apparently had fallen out of his back pocket when he went to the bathroom and then had been flushed. Fortunately, the package was too big to fit through the hole. I had to scape them out of the toilet and carefully pull them apart so they could dry.

When Lewis arrived home the next day, he saw the checks laid out on towels all over the kitchen, but to his credit he knew better than to ask what had happened. He may have figured it out later, however, when he went to use his toilet and found a hairnet stretched across the opening to catch any valuables that might fall from his pants pockets as he ascended his throne.

Another of Lewis' bad habits was his smoking, which he has done on and off since I've known him. Whenever he was "on," he was *never* without a pack of cigarettes. If he was ever caught without, it was best to vacate the area.

One winter night when it was sleeting outside, he sat down to write a column only to discover he'd misplaced his cigarettes. He was doubly furious because he had just bought a new pack and knew they were around somewhere. He rummaged through all his pants and jacket pockets and sent me outside to search the car and the driveway between the garage and back door, but we could not find them.

Next he started looking in garbage cans all over the house. "Lewis," I said, "how could they have gotten into a garbage can?"

"I've given up on those. I'm looking for a good butt to puff on, but you're so damned spick-and-span I can't even find one."

I apologized for emptying his ash trays and offered him an alternative butt to put his lips on.

Finally I decided it was better to risk life and limb by driving through the sleet to buy another pack than to sit around listening to Lewis imitate the sounds of a Lamaze class as he went cold turkey.

Barney the basset hound performing his best trick

I returned half an hour later to find him in front of his typewriter enveloped in a cloud of smoke. When I asked where he had found his cigarettes, he answered nonchalantly and without looking up, "In the refrigerator where I left them when I put up my six-pack of beer." Perfectly logical.

The loss of his wallet was usually an easier mystery to solve. Most times it was either stuck in the crack of his car seat, on a bench at the tennis center, or in the washing machine. He never had any money in his wallet because he kept his bills rolled up in sweaty little balls in his pockets. So the only things of value left in his wallet were his press pass, his card with the seven early warning signs of cancer, and his driver's license, which had been washed so many times his photo looked like Sirhan Sirhan.

I tried to remember to frisk everybody's clothes before I washed, but sometimes I forgot. Once I washed Lewis' tennis shorts and T-shirts with a load of the kids' stuff. As I pulled them out to put in the dryer, I gasped. There were kaleidoscopic colors covering his pastel shorts and formerly white shirts. I couldn't figure out what in the world had happened until I discovered in my six-year-old son's pockets the bulk of his nursery school's chalk and crayon supply.

When Lewis saw what had happened, he was unusually understanding: "You've ruined my life!" he screamed. "I can't go out on a tennis court looking like a Peter Max poster!" And then, for good measure, he added, "This never *used* to happen."

"Very true," I said in self-defense. "Colors don't run when they're never washed."

Sometimes good things happened when I washed Lewis' clothes, like "Drying for Dollars." As I said earlier, he always balled up his paper money and stuffed it in his pants pockets. After doing the laundry, I'd open the dryer and lots of nice, warm bills would fall out.

At first I felt bad about taking his "laundered money," but as it continued, I started counting on it. The amounts varied depending on where he had been the night before. After a poker game, particularly when he had won, I was in the money because the dozen beers he had consumed the night before made him forget how much money he had. After a night on the town with the boys, "Drying for Dollars" was better than a slot machine in Las Vegas. Sometimes I could collect up to seventy-five dollars in a single cycle. I figured I had earned every cent of it.

Lewis enjoyed arguing and did so with me often. I think it gave him a chance to say all the things he couldn't say in the newspaper. One of our most popular subjects for arguing was the mysterious disappearance of his socks. He would accuse me of "letting" the washing machine eat them, or he would say that the housekeeper was stealing them one at a time, or he would accuse me of holding them for "ransom" to slowly drive him crazy. (It would have been a short trip.)

Inevitably the socks would show up stuck to somebody's underwear or to one of my silk nighties. But the most dramatic reappearance of a missing sock was the notorious "Barney Incident."

One Saturday morning we had a particularly bad fight about one of his new, over-the-calf, black Christian Dior socks being missing. He was furious that *one* of a brand new pair was already gone, and he accused me of being responsible. Then he huffed off to the tennis courts, announcing over his shoulder that he would be home late in the afternoon with the entire team for a party, since it was the last match of the season.

When they arrived that afternoon, I was still rather cool towards him because of the fight, but he and the gang were all laughs since they had won the championship. I finally joined them on the patio, and Barney wandered over to see what all the commotion was about.

The guys were replaying all the big points of the day, guzzling beer, and slapping each other on the back. Right in the middle of the party, however, Barney walked over to the edge of the patio and started to do his buiness. It's bad enough that your dog would "drop a card" right on the patio in front of a crowd, but old Barn made it worse by straining and groaning.

Slowly the source of the problem appeared . . . and kept appearing until the Dior monogram was visible.

Like the guys on the team, I suddenly enjoyed "the thrill of victory." Old Barn had vindicated me.

HAVE WE ALWAYS HAD
GREEN SHAG CARPET IN THE CLOSET?

I don't claim to be a "neatnik," but I do like things in their place — sort of organized clutter. And I will vacuum and dust if threatened with a visit from my mother or the Avon lady. But living with Lewis was a new experience — sort of like combining "Hints From Heloise" with a HUD project.

Am I implying that Lewis was a slob? You bet your upright Hoover, I am.

I had seen his house before we were married and knew the sanitation department was investigating him for operating an illegal landfill, but I thought after we got married he would take enough pride in our home to keep it a little cleaner. Yeah, and Gloria Steinem would be his next wife, too.

When Lewis came in from playing tennis, he would begin dropping sweaty clothes at the back door and then leave a trail all the way to the bedroom. He particularly liked to drop wet towels on the hardwood floors and soaking wristbands on the upholstered chairs. I guess it was like Hansel and Gretel — he wanted to be able to find his way back out of the house.

He would finally arrive in the bedroom and throw whatever else was left on the floor of his closet and then close the door. I wouldn't find these articles until a week later when they had become UCO (Unidentifiable Closet Objects). You could comb what was growing off the top of them, and the rest could have been harvested to feed several hundred Richard Simmons devotees. We grew sprouts, mushrooms, some tofu-looking stuff, and once I even found a little family of snails living in a sock.

In order to clean this out, I would get a rake, a heavy-duty leaf and lawn bag, and the trusty shower cap I had pilfered from the Ritz-Carlton Hotel. I would tie the shower cap on the front of my face like a mask, go into the closet and scrape the amoebic growth into the bag, tie it up, label it with a skull and crossbones, and drag it out to the street hoping that it wouldn't detonate along the way.

Now that I think back on it, some of those missing socks probably just rotted away in the back of his closet.

SICK BY ASSOCIATION . . . OR IMAGINATION

Lewis often suffered from insomnia, but given his fear of doctors, he would do nothing to alleviate it. He preferred instead to complain about it all night. According to him, he had never had a good night's sleep in his life, and it infuriated him to no end that I could drop right off.

We would get into bed at night, and he'd find the slightest excuse for not being able to sleep — the walls in the bedroom were too white, I breathed too loudly while I slept, the shadows on the trees outside the window made a design on the ceiling that looked like the Shroud of Turin, and so forth.

He had some sleeping pills but refused to take them because he said they didn't do any good. Of course, he'd never actually tried them, but he just knew they wouldn't work.

Occasionally I would ask if he thought the dozen beers he had guzzled throughout the evening contributed in any way to his insomnia, and this would send him into a rage. "That's easy for you to say, Miss Kitty van Winkle." Then he'd go on to lecture me about the virtues of a good wife, insisting that if I were one, I'd stay awake all night to suffer along with him and give him somebody to talk to.

Quite by accident one night, I came upon a temporary cure for Lewis' insomnia. The kids were in bed, and I was watching a blood and guts thriller on the VCR (my favorite entertainment; I love scaring myself silly by watching through spread fingers as people get chain-sawed, strangled till their eyeballs pop out, axed and stuck on a door, hanged, drowned, or generally mutilated. I still think Friday the Thirteenth should have won an Academy Award). Lewis came in from a speech and sat down beside me. In less than fifteen minutes, he was sound asleep.

Even though he spent the night on the sofa, he slept straight until morning. He tried to tell me he didn't sleep a wink, but I assured him that his telltale snoring and drooling were non-stop throughout my marathon movie night.

I wasn't sure if it was late-night movies in general or just horror movies that put him to sleep, so I tried it the next night with one of my favorite dramas, Witness for the Prosecution. But Lewis got so involved in the movie that he was up all night arguing about Tyrone Power's innocence. I immediately joined the "Monster of the Month" club at the local video store, so I would be assured of getting the newest ghoulish release and Lewis would be assured of getting an occasional night of sleep.

Despite their gory content, these films never gave Lewis nightmares. Instead, he dreamed of being trapped in frustrating situations. Once he dreamed that his typewriter came alive in his office, and as he leaned over to replace the ribbon, the ampersand reached up and grabbed him, pulled his face down close to the bar, and rolled his lips around it as if they were a piece of paper. He was stuck there until his faithful secretary showed up to release him. What really irritated him about this dream was that the editor of the paper had walked by, witnessed Lewis caught in his lip lock, and just kept on walking.

In another of his dreams, he was in a barnyard and all the animals were talking about him. They accused him of being a bigot because he never had anything nice to say about the ducks. He tried to hide in the barn, but they found him and asked if he wanted to defend himself against the charge. If he had no defense, they were going to sentence him to a life of hard labor mucking out the mules' stalls and acting as midwife to all the rabbits. The frustration was that when he opened his mouth to tell of his great love for ducks and geese, nothing came out. He was mute. Thus the occupants of Old McDonald's farm carried out their punishment.

This dream puzzled him for days, and he kept trying to figure out the symbolism involved. Finally he didn't talk about it anymore, but a new bumper sticker appeared on his car saying, "Ducks Count."

One of the worst effects of Lewis' insomnia was his mood the next morning. I would be up and getting the kids off to school when, according to Lewis, he was just getting to sleep. The slightest noise would bother him, so we had to slip around very quietly. On the mornings that I had to take the kids to school, I tried to remember to take the phone off the hook. But sometimes I forgot.

One of my family members would call and awaken the dragon in his lair.

"Mornin', Lewis, is Kathy there?"

"Gone to take the kids to school," he would growl, and then he'd slam the phone down with such force that it would make the caller's eyes spin like fruit in a slot machine.

Another time an unsuspecting friend called and got the "heavy breather hang-up treatment," which was Lewis picking up the phone, listening to the voice on the other end, realizing it wasn't for him, and hanging up.

But the saddest were the strangers who would call and innocently ask for Mrs. Grizzard. Lewis wouldn't hang up on them right away. Instead, he would torture them with a clever sort of banter by asking why they hadn't called a rooster if they wanted to talk so early in the morning, or, hadn't they read the etiquette books stating that it was impolite to phone anyone before eleven in the morning?

I was amused one day when Lewis complained that we had been receiving some harrassing phone calls. I asked him what he meant, and he said people had been calling the house early in the morning and hanging up. I was glad my friends and family were finally catching on.

JUST ADD WATER AND . . . YOU'RE A FATHER

Lewis has never been known for his patience, but few things got to him quicker than children. In our case, of course, he married into a couple of them. His lack of tolerance may result from being an only child, although he claimed that he was *never* a child himself.

He firmly believed in the philosophy that children (and most times wives) should be seen and not heard, and even the "seen" should be on a limited scale.

After reading *Rise and Fall of the Third Reich* and *The Nightmare Years*, Lewis decided that he knew everything there was to know about discipline. He called my children in and explained that ours was not a democratic home but a bureaucratic one, and that he was the omnipotent ruler.

"Any questions?" he asked.

Bruce, the six-year-old, nodded yes.

"OK, take one step forward and speak up," ordered Lewis.

Bruce stepped forward as directed and then replied, "Mom said you're not supposed to say words like omnipplent in front of us."

Dr. Adolf Spock just shook his head and dismissed the troops.

Discipline wasn't the only thing about Lewis the kids didn't understand. They weren't exactly sure what their new daddy did for a living. They knew he wrote funny stories, but they didn't know the difference between his typed pages and a magazine or a newspaper, and that misunderstanding once led to quite an embarrassment.

One Friday night, daughter Lisa found a *Playboy* magazine in Lewis' office at home. She quickly alerted her brother, and they absconded with it . . .

unbeknownst to their mother. When I went to tuck them in later, I found them convulsing with laughter under the covers. I grabbed the magazine away, smacked them both on the bottom, and told them never to go into Lewis' office again. Then I pulled out the big stick: "I'm sure Lewis will have something to say to you about this when he gets home."

When he arrived a short time later, I said, "You go in there and tell them that someone gave you that magazine by accident, and that you *never* read such trash, and that if you ever catch them in your office again you'll spank them both.

"OK," he said, "but I don't know what the big deal is."

He went into their room and I heard him say, "Hey, kids. Your mom tells me you found a dirty magazine in my office. You know you're never supposed to go in there anyway, but since you did, I'm writing an article about something in that *Playboy* and had to read it. I don't look at the pictures. Now go to sleep."

Lisa and Bruce stifled their laughter, but after Lewis left the room they decided to draw their own *Playboy* magazine with crayons and construction paper.

Unfortunately, I didn't find out about the X-rated artwork until a week later. The following Friday was "Show and Tell" time in Bruce's class at school. So he took his own version of *Playboy*, showed it to the class and announced, "My daddy, Lewis, writes funny stories for this magazine, but my mom wouldn't let me bring the real one."

His teacher tried to calm me by saying that regardless of the subject, stick people just weren't very sensual.

Lewis and I had another disagreement about parenting the day he came home and found Lisa trying to pass off her younger brother as her friend Buffy. She introduced Lewis to this kid with a ribbon in his hair, wearing leotards and tights, and with nail polish on his fingers. "Buffy" did a little pirouette and curtsied for "her" stepdad.

At first Lewis paid slight attention, but when they started dancing, he realized that the kid was in fact Bruce in Lisa's ballet clothes. He was outraged and blamed me for their aberrant behavior. He accused me of raising a six-year-old drag queen "who belongs on a float at Carnival in Rio," and told me I should discipline them. For punishment, he suggested that I play pitch with Bruce for an hour a day for the next week to remind him of his gender.

Several months later, Lewis became extremely concerned that Bruce was always scratching his rear end. "Everytime I look at him," he said, "he's got his hand stuck down the back of his pants." And then, to Bruce, "What's the matter, boy, you cut the seat outta your britches and let the gnats in?"

Bruce continued to scratch until finally Lewis could stand it no longer, so I took my son to the doctor. Calmly but surely, the doctor said he had pinworms. I hadn't heard of those nasty little things since my sisters and I got them as kids from running around barefoot during the summer. But the remedy was still the same — sulphur tablets for the afflicted *and* for the rest of the family. I knew that was going to be a hard pill to swallow for Lewis.

That night at dinner I said, "I took Bruce to the doctor today, and he has worms, so we all have to take this medicine." Then I handed him a little pink pill.

"My God, Kitty, don't tell me that while I'm trying to eat. Besides, *I* don't have any worms. I haven't even been fishing lately."

"Nice try, Lew, but you don't get them from handling bait," I said.

"Well, I ain't taking no pill," he said adamantly.

"Fine," I countered, "but you'd better start carrying a box of Hartz Mountain wormer in your tennis bag so that when the little buggers start crawling out of your shorts you can kill them."

All the time I was speaking, he was making exaggerated retching noises, which meant he didn't want to hear any more of my "worms of wisdom." We finished dinner in silence, but when he left the table, he discreetly dropped the pink pill in his pocket.

WHAT KIND OF TOOL AM I?

When it came to help around the house, Lewis was help*less*. He had absolutely no mechanical aptitude. None. He could study a used-up typewriter ribbon for hours and still have trouble putting in a new one.

Lewis has written many times that he keeps his old Royal manual typewriter as a matter of principal — "That's the way stories are supposed to be written" — but the truth is that he could never figure out how to work an electric typewriter and certainly not a word processor. The entire IBM training staff couldn't make him proficient. And the first time a message flashed on the screen telling him he had made an error, he'd smash in the screen.

Once my kitchen sink was leaking and (before I knew better) I asked Lewis to take a look to see if he could find the problem. He poked around under the sink for about thirty minutes, but it was still leaking.

When the kids came in for dinner and saw him under the sink, Lisa said, "Better call Mr. Goodwrench, Mom." To which Lewis replied in earnest, "We don't need any candy bars right now. We're fixing to have dinner."

I stuck a bucket under the sink until the plumber could come the next day. The problem turned out to be an loose nut. Took him five minutes and cost forty dollars.

Another time we had a flood in the basement, so I called the same plumber. He told me over the phone that we needed a sump pump and that I could save money by getting one before he arrived. When I told Lewis that night that we needed a sump pump and asked if he knew where to get one, he said, "I guess the drugstore. Isn't that where you usually buy a laxative?"

Such simple chores as hanging pictures, putting up a shower curtain, and cranking the lawnmower were monumental tasks for Lewis. One year for Christmas I gave him a book entitled, *Anyone Can Do It*, a fix-it manual. He seemed genuinely pleased to get it, but he never opened it the first time. Several months later I found it in the back of a file drawer. Stuck in the middle of the book, in a section called "Taking the Plunge With Your Plumber's Friend . . . Tough Toilet Talk," were copies of his past divorce decrees.

I gave up after that and told him he would have to budget for household repair. It was easier to hire people than to teach Lewis the fundamentals of survival in that jungle known as "the home."

Europe On A Concierge A Day

My love for travel developed early, back in the days of the "Woody" station wagon and endless family trips down the hot, dusty, two-laned highways to Florida. My dad was not usually along for these "treks through Hell," as I once heard my mother describe them. He would fly down later and meet us. So that left Mom as custodian of four girls fighting like alley cats in the "wayback."

Since it was an eleven-hour drive and had to be made in one day, Mom did not like to stop if she could help it. She solved the food and drink problem by packing a cooler with a picnic lunch, which we would finish by the time we reached the city limits or by 8 A.M., whichever came first.

The bathroom problem was handled with equal

dispatch. Four little girls chugging Bireley's grape, orange, and chocolate drinks needed "relief" every fifteen minutes, so we carried a metal pot and used it. We became experts at emptying the pot out of a partially rolled-down window. Before long, of course, we weren't content to merely empty the pot. We needed a target.

Our plan was simple: wait for a passing car and let 'em have it. My sisters were the lookouts, and I was chosen executioner of "Mission Wet."

A black Cadillac Coupe de Ville was first to appear out of the haze of heat rising from the blacktop road. My sister Helen began the countdown, and I hoisted the pot onto the ledge of the fully rolled-down window. As the car began to pass us, I heard, "2 . . . 1 . . . 0 . . . pitch it!" I extended my body like "Elastic Lass" in my comic books, and my sisters grabbed hold of my ankles for safety sake. I flung the contents of the metal latrine and scored a direct hit on the windshield.

As the car continued to pass us, the perturbed driver gave our unsuspecting mother the finger and mouthed a lot of bad words to her. She couldn't hear him because of the wind rushing by, but she got the gist of his message and pulled over to the side of the road. She took one look at my wet clothes and the smirks on all our faces and removed her belt. We didn't even get to pick our own switches.

From then on, a lot of the thrill was gone where our portable potty was concerned, so we went back to fighting and looking at the pictures of natives in Dad's *National Geographics*.

In spite of the long, hot rides, I loved those trips. The education was invaluable, and I was left with memories that still give me pleasure. How could I forget our stops at B. Lloyd's, Stuckeys, Jungle World, Alligator Alley, Indian Moccasin Mountain, Reptile City, Spook Swamp, Beach Towel Bonanza, Sunken Gardens, Cypress Gardens, and the incomparable Weeki-Wachi Springs? I loved those beautiful mermaids who sucked air from tubes hidden beneath the rocks. I was jealous of their lovely bathing beauty figures, for I was in that pudgy stage. I consoled myself by watching the goosepimples form on their arms sometimes and loved it when one of them had a great purple bruise on a thigh.

Another thing I enjoyed about travelling was experiencing different hotels and restaurants. I was fascinated with decor, service, and the preparation of food in which I did not play a part. I loved telling someone else to bring me a Ho-Jo and a 3-D burger and, in later years, requesting that my pheasant be just a touch on the pink side. My hotel preferences also changed dramatically as I got older and continued to travel. I went from being content with the adequate surroundings at Howard Johnson's as a child to savoring the elegance of the Hassler in Rome as a more discerning adult.

Lewis and I travelled together a great deal. His work and speeches kept him on the road constantly, and I was our designated tour director. After a couple of years of putting up with his travel quirks (and they were numerous), I decided I could arrange trips for anyone, so I went into the travel business. My timing was good, because by then we were divorced and I *needed* a job.

I learned very quickly that being a travel advisor/counselor/agent was a short route to a sure-fire nervous breakdown, and one reason was having to deal with prima donna male travellers.

They could be travelling on business or pleasure, alone or with a companion, but however they went, it was very important to them that *I* knew they had been everywhere, done everything, and that they would direct my doltish attempts at arranging their travel. They would talk to me as though I had just escaped from the Yerkes Primate Center, and if perchance I happened to suggest a particular hotel or destination they approved of, it was by sheer accident. These men assumed that I had never been anywhere, was never going anywhere, and lived in my office for the sole purpose of waiting on them.

Since they considered my mentality a fluke of nature, they also presumed that I could not figure out when they were sneaking off with some angora-brained half-wit and leaving their wives at home to paint the garage.

They always came in with the same sleazy grin and upbeat greeting: "Hey, sweetheart, what's happenin'?" What's happening is that your anchovy breath just melted the wires on the back of my computer, and no, I don't want to book you and Pepper in the No-Tell Hotel for the week. But since my boss insisted on making money before she paid

The happy traveler in front of Westminster Abbey

me, I would sit there in my convincing moronic state and take directions:

"My friend (or lady or companion — these terms were never used when referring to wives) and I want a one-bedroom cottage on the ground level, ocean front side, king-sized bed with overhead fan, twenty-four-hour room service available from a private valet, tropicana roses by the bed, jacuzzi surrounded by mirrors, his and her terry-cloth robes, video cassette recorder with camera, and a refrig-o-bar stocked with Dom Perignon, Beluga caviar, and some snow crab claws. Pepper just *adores* crab." Good, I thought, I hope she'll give you some.

In comparison, the penny-pinching married man travelling with his wife had only three requests: "Gimme the cheapest room in the cheapest motel and single beds, 'cause she snores." I often asked these tightwads why they didn't treat their wives to a little surprise and upgrade the room a bit, and I'd have some flowers or fruit awaiting them. They would respond, "We'll never be in the room. Why do I care what it looks like?"

But if you think working with a macho globetrotter is tough, travelling with him is even worse. I once had to go to New York with my boss and her husband on business. He was Mr. Big Apple (B.A.) — knew everything there was to know about the teeming metropolis. He delighted in directing cabbies on the best routes to take.

One morning we came out of our hotel, The Plaza on Fifth Avenue, and had the doorman hail a cab for us. We all got in the back and Mr. B.A. said, "G.M. Building!"

"What?" said the cabbie.

Mr. B.A. roared in a sonic boom voice, "I said, G.M. Building!"

"OK, buddy, you got it." And with whiplash speed, the cab roared off from the front of the Plaza, made a U-turn on Fifth Avenue, and pulled up directly on the opposite side of the street in front of the G.M. Building. Mr. B.A. tipped the smiling driver and got out as though nothing unusual had happened.

I'M STICKING LIKE GLUE TO YOU, BABE

Lewis' travel demands weren't too extreme within the United States. Good food and good service usually would make him happy, and these were pretty easy to come by. Once over the Atlantic, however, he became an "ugly American." His patience was nil and mine was stretched thin . . . by him.

The first time we went to Europe, I told Lewis that I would take care of all the arrangements. All he had to do was pack a suitcase and accompany me to the airport. That was easier said than done.

I luckily inspected his suitcase before we zipped it and was shocked by the contents. He had put in three pairs of tennis shorts, a floral bathing suit, a six-pack of Tab, an eight-volume history of the Second World War which he had ordered off television, a spotting scope that Galileo would have been proud of, and his hairdryer. That suitcase could not have been lifted with a crane. I repacked for him, reverting to the Granimal system which had been effective earlier in our relationship.

When making plans for our trip, I had asked Lewis if he had any special requests concerning hotels.

"No, I just don't want to stay in no hotel where they've had any goats and chickens," he said. For some reason he thought we were going on a jaunt through eastern Europe and were going to "rough it." *Au contraire.* He should have known me better.

As I said earlier, I like my accommodations while travelling to be aesthetically pleasing. It is important to me that a hotel room be large and comfortable, and, of course, a private bath is an absolute necessity. But I was suprised to discover that such rooms and the attendant amenities were also important to Lewis.

He loved the hand-and-foot service in European hotels ("I never get this kind of treatment at home!"). That is, he loved it when he could ask for it, but he often had trouble communicating his desires. It irritated him to no end that all Europeans did not speak English. Of course, he saw nothing at all wrong with the fact that he didn't speak any foreign language. "I'm the tourist here. They're supposed to cater to me," he said.

Then one day I told him about concierges.

"What's that, another one of those smelly French cheeses?" he said.

I explained that concierges at luxury hotels were at his disposal for sending telex, telegrams, making reservations at restaurants or the theater, car or limosine rentals, guide services, and any general problems. They all spoke English, so he would be easily understood.

"Sounds good," he said. "I'll give it a try."

He marched up to the concierge desk at our Paris hotel, the swank Crillon, and said, "'Scuse me, monsoon, but could you get me a couple of barbecue pork pig sandwiches and send 'em to my room?"

I nearly fainted, but the man at the counter smiled politely and said if we would check in first, he would see what he could do later.

So we checked in, got our room assigned, and were handed a key. Not just any key — a key that looked like an intricate brass battering ram, and on one end was a huge purple tassel, similar to the one Beulah the Three-Breasted Woman used to twirl at the Great Southeastern Fair. Lewis asked the desk clerk if it came with a wheelbarrow for hauling it around, but fortunately the man didn't understand.

We were shown to our room, and after the embarrassment of watching Lewis try to figure the tip in francs, we were left alone to examine our lavish facilities. Lewis immediately found the phone and started punching buttons for the services he could figure out from the symbols. Then he flipped through the room service menus and began marking his selections, all the while searching for the barbecue special.

He turned on the television but was surprised to find every program in French. "You'd figure they would at least provide subtitles," he complained. Then he picked up the phone again, dialed the concierge, and said, "Hey, Bud, when you send up those barbecue pork pig sandwiches, tell the fellow to bring along an English-speaking television."

When I got the phone away from him, we continued our tour. The bathroom was big and plush with lots of mirrors, and Lewis was particularly impressed that the toilet was in a room by itself. Then he spotted the bidet. "Look, Kitty, we got a two-holer!" He went over to it and reenacted Old Faithful by turning on the spigot as hard as it would go.

I explained to him as clearly as I could the function of the bidet, and from then on he referred to it as the "Magical French Fanny Fountain."

Lewis was having to write his newspaper columns throughout our trip, and dealing with that pressure, plus the confusion of different time zones, left him tightly strung. Another way to say it is that his temperament was reminiscent of Hitler with hemorrhoids. Therefore, we argued about the most trivial things.

One memorable disagreement occurred the night before we left Paris and led to the infamous "Train Station Massacre" the following morning.

We were supposed to entertain some business friends with dinner at world-famous Maxim's. Lewis was running late with his column, so he told me to go ahead and he'd meet me at the restaurant. Before leaving, I gave myself a manicure and used some Krazy Glue to repair a broken nail. I was in a bit of a hurry, so I left the tube of glue on the glass top of the coffee table where I had been working.

Lewis finished his column, took a shower, and reluctantly put on the tuxedo and frilly shirt I had laying out for him on the bed. As he was about to leave the room, he spotted the tube of glue on the coffee table and — in an uncharacteristically neat gesture — went to pick it up and move it. Of course, it was stuck firmly to the table. For some reason, this set him off.

He pulled and tugged and cussed at the tube, but as anyone who has ever seen that man hanging from his hardhat on TV knows, it wasn't giving. In frustration he took a letter opener from the desk and tried to pry the tube loose. Instead it broke in two, sending a quick spurt of glue out all over Lewis' hands and fingers. Now he had a new problem. His hands were like paddles, which is fine if you're going swimming but not good if you're on your way to Maxim's in a tuxedo.

Lewis washed and scraped and bit and finally got enough glue off to at least separate his fingers, and then he headed for the restaurant . . . in a rage.

I saw him enter the formal dining room where we were seated amidst patrons representative of Old-World elegance. Chandelier crystals tinkled and sparkled from the candlelight on the tables below as the maitre d' showed Lewis to our table. I was impressed with how handsome he looked in his tuxedo, even though the effect was lessened some-what by the telltale tassel of our room key dangling from his pants pocket.

As he sat down, he gave me a look so chilling it could have turned Charles Manson into Pat Boone. He made some mild attempts at light banter as we tried to visit with the lovely English couple we were entertaining, but the Captain Queeg-type motions he kept making with his fingers indicated unrest. Of course, I didn't know at the time that he was actually rolling glue balls off his hands throughout what seemed our never-ending dinner.

When we said good-bye to our guests and walked out the restaurant door, he immediately started in about the glue. "How could anyone purchase a (ex-pletive deleted) chemical over the (ditto) counter so strong it could have glued the (again) Titanic back together if they'd had it on board? And you, you put it on your (same) fingers! What's wrong with you?"

I told him he should be proud that I was trying to look nice for him. "If you wanted to be seen in Maxim's with a woman who looked like she'd been digging beets all day, then you should have married Mother Theresa!" He said he wished he had.

That did it. The fight was on. I knew I was no verbal match for Lewis, so I went into my "zipper lip *modus vivendi*" (which translates into "the silent treatment"). This was particularly hard to do while travelling in a foreign country, because it makes hailing taxis or porters, tipping, and asking direc-tions very difficult. However, the next morning in the Paris train station, Lewis was still lecturing on glue and I was still mute.

We were running late, as usual, and couldn't find a porter, so we had to load all our luggage on a pushcart and wheel it down to the train by ourselves. This was no easy feat, since our luggage rivaled Barnum and Bailey's after a tour. I grabbed the cart's handle to push it, and Lewis — not seeing my fingers between the cart and the handle — did the same thing. He squeezed the handle to release the brake and in the process crushed my fingers and smashed the fingernails I had pampered the night before. I screamed in agony and stared at my flat and ridged fingers.

When I had regained my composure, I spoke to him just long enough to vow — in quite loud and colorful language — never to speak to him again. I came close.

We travelled many miles in silence and even crossed the English Channel without speaking. I would have spoken to someone other than Lewis, but that was impossible because the entire Hovercraft was filled with Japanese tourists. When we landed at the cliffs of Dover, Lewis said loudly, "I bleeve that gentleman driving this vibrating carwash took a wrong turn and landed us at a Kodak convention in Okinawa." I hated him then for his humor and had to turn away to stifle a laugh.

When we reached the station at Moreton on the Marsh, a beautiful village in the English countryside, our friend Peter was waiting for us just as planned. To add more magic to the storybook scene, he had come to pick us up in a wonderful old Alvis convertible. Peter and Lewis put our luggage in the trunk while I stopped to look at some unusual wild-flowers growing by the side of the train station. As Peter locked the trunk, Lewis walked around to the right side of the car and climbed in. I heard Peter say, "Driving are you, old chap?" Lewis jumped out and headed around the front of the car to the other side . . . the one without the steering wheel.

On his way around, however, he stepped in some fresh dog doo hidden among the leaves. He spent an embarrassing next few minutes trying to scrape it off his Guccis — first on the grass, then on the curb, and finally with a stick. I climbed in the front seat and laughed till I cried.

Finally I couldn't resist any longer. I had to speak: "That stuff is worse than Krazy Glue, isn't it Lew?"

A ROME WITH A VIEW

By the time we reached Italy, Lewis was a veteran traveller. The first thing he did whenever we checked into a hotel was grease the palm of the concierge. I had unknowingly created a monster.

We had only three days to spend in Rome, and Lewis insisted that he didn't want to spend the whole time sightseeing. "We should be able to hit the high spots in a day," he said.

I balked. "Rome is an enormous city. Why would you want to cram all its beauty and history into one day?"

"Kitty," he said, "when you've seen one statue of a naked man you've seen them all. Besides, I've already lined up a tour guide with the concierge."

The tour guide turned out to be the concierge's cousin, who probably worked nights with the Red Brigade. And instead of the limosine I had envisioned, he picked us up in a tiny Fiat whose back seat was so small it was almost the front seat.

Marcello took us first to Vatican City and St. Peter's Cathedral. Lewis was unimpressed with the grandeur of the structure, but he was fascinated by the Popes who were buried there. "Look at these little shrunk-up Popes. They sure was little folks, weren't they?" Then as we were leaving, which was about fifteen minutes after we had arrived, Lewis blurted out, "Hey, wait a minute. I think we missed something important. Where is that King Tut's grave? He was one of them little guys too, wasn't he?"

From there we headed for the Colosseum, after a stop along the way for Lewis and Marcello to stock up on beer. As we sped around the Arch of Constantine, Marcello thrilled Lewis by telling him he had been in the movie *Ben-Hur*. He was an extra in the famed chariot race scene.

"All right!" Lewis screamed. "That was one hell of a movie! Hey, what was it like having to wear that short, sissy, leather dress in public?"

In broken English, Marcello said, "It no worse than those plaid pants you wearing."

We continued our whirlwind tour of Rome with Marcello offering less-than-interesting tidbits of history. Occasionally he would ask if we wanted to get out at a particular point of interest to get a closer look, but Lewis invariably said it was too hot.

Three miserable hours later, we pulled up in front of the hotel and I bolted. As I ran through the door, I heard the fading sounds of Lewis saying to his new buddy Marcello, "Now try it once more. And remember, it's *Glory! Glory!* to old Georgia, not *Gory! Gory!*"

Marcello must have been pleased with Lewis' tip, because he gave him a coupon good for a complimentary "kneecapping." Two years later when we were divorced, I found that coupon and destroyed it.

One day in Florence, that stunningly beautiful city on the Arno River, we went shopping. Lewis, you'll remember, bought Guccis and three ascots. I found a lovely pair of Italian leather boots, but Lewis was so impatient, I barely had time to try them on before I bought them. I decided to wear them out of the store and break them in.

We walked around until lunchtime, sat for an hour or two in Harry's Bar, and then shopped for another couple of hours. We were both exhausted, so we decided to order dinner in our room. I began to undress to shower before dinner, but I couldn't get my new boots off. I pulled and twisted, but they wouldn't budge.

Finally I got Lewis to try, and he gave a feeble yank and nothing happened. My feet were so swollen from the afternoon of walking that there was no way I could get those boots off. So, while I was writhing on the floor still trying, Lewis did what any considerate husband would do — he called the concierge.

In his best Italian accent, he said, "Signor, could you send-o somebody to take off the boot-os of my wife-o?"

I was horrified! No one was going to look up my skirt and pull my boots off.

The charming Italian concierge sent one of his assistants to check out the problem with the Americans and their boots in Room 565. I hid in the bathroom and lied, saying that I had gotten them off.

The boots were henceforth known as my "sleepin' boots," because that's what I had to do in them that night. They did not come off until the next morning when the swelling had gone down.

I hoped we could check out of our hotel without having to face the concierge after the boot incident, but no such luck. While I was finally freeing my feet from the boots, Lewis went into the bathroom, and before I could say "Reddy Kilowatt," he had turned on his hairdryer without using the electrical converter.

The dryer became a fiery ray gun. It smoked and flamed, and I finally had to jump on the cord to disconnect it. All the fuses in our room and the rooms next to us were blown. I was willing just to sneak out of the hotel at that point, but they already knew too much about us.

Lewis again called the concierge, explained the

problem, and asked if they had another hairdryer he could borrow. (The man was downright shameless at times.) The concierge sent up a parade of five men to begin work on the electrical problems, and one of them brought a hairdryer, which Lewis had to go down a flight to use since that was the nearest available power.

A TIP? PLANT YOUR CORN
EARLY THIS YEAR

Money exchange and conversion was another area where Lewis was often confused and depended on concierges for help. Rather than go to the bank where rates were lowest, he would pay whatever the going hotel rate was just so he didn't have to "talk to strangers." Unfortunately, the concierge usually wasn't around when it came time to tip.

I would offer suggestions on what I thought was an appropriate tip in certain situations, but Lewis would just stuff some bills in the hand of a bellboy, waiter, porter, or maid. He thought as long as it was paper, it was enough.

Once in Italy while travelling by train, we were amused when a porter dropped to his knees, grabbed the hand of a rather dapper-looking older gentleman, and began kissing it. I went up to the man and asked what was going on, and he said, "All I did was give the guy a tip . . . obviously it was too much." Conversely, on a train from Paris to Lyon late one night, Lewis and I frantically looked around for a porter as we pulled into the station. Before the train could even stop, I jumped out and grabbed the only one in sight. He had a cart and somehow managed to drag all our luggage about a quarter of a mile down to the station. In appreciation for this service, old "Michelin Grizzard" reached deep into his pants and pulled out a wad of paper bills. He handed the porter some English pounds, some German deutsche marks, and about seventy-five cents in French francs.

I thought the man was going to smack Lewis. He was yelling uncontrollably. I quickly reached for my Berlitz as Lewis dug into his pockets, pulling out anything he could find — movie stubs, paper clips, passport, train tickets, but no more money. Finally, in my worst French and according to the only thing I could find applicable in my Berlitz book, I said, "*Il est bête*," which roughly means, "He is dumb." Then I added, "*Bête comme un chou!*" which I hoped meant, "As stupid as a cabbage!"

The porter looked back at Lewis, still clawing in his pockets, and then smiled at me. I handed him a few U.S. dollars, which further appeased him.

When we were safe, Lewis asked what I had said to calm "that mad Frenchman."

"In a nutshell, I just told him that all your pastries weren't puffed."

IF THE BUN FITS, EAT IT

Ordering food abroad was a continual challenge with Lewis because I never knew what would show up on his plate. One thing I did know was that it would not be what he thought he had ordered.

Occasionally he would be bold enough to try pronouncing what he wanted — his *profiterole* usually came out "profit roll" — but most times he just pointed. Once in a German railroad station, even that got him in trouble. His pointing apparently confused our waitress, and the fraulein brought him "a foot-long weenie" and a round hard roll.

Lewis tried to explain that the shapes weren't right — they didn't go together. What he needed was two things that were tubular or two things that were round, but not one of each. The waitress did not grasp his gyrations, which bordered on being obscene as he tried to show her what kind of bun went with a weenie. He finally gave up, drank a few more beers, and spent the next half hour trying to roll up his weenie like a snake and put it in the round bun. One of the ends would always slip out and slap him in the face, leaving a big string of mustard hanging off his mustache.

Another time we were driving with some friends through the beautiful Loire Valley in France on a tour of the château region. Lewis was in a particularly jubilant mood because the couple with us had announced their engagement that very afternoon. To celebrate, we had stopped at a quaint little shop in Chartres and bought some cheese, bread, and champagne.

After about two hours and three bottles of celebration, Lewis was primed.

We arrived at our château just in time for dinner.

After checking in and unpacking, the four of us headed for the dining room, where we were greeted by the charming hostess who was also the owner of the château. She escorted us to a lovely table overlooking the garden.

Lewis, who was still feeling no pain, started nodding off the minute we were seated. He would occasionally jerk his head up and snort, then drop it again and begin to drool. I thought he was too far gone to hear Madame Tortier's description of the specialties, but unfortunately he wasn't.

"Tonight's speciality," she began with the grace of royalty, "is a lovely head of calf, served in a delicate wine sauce with brains and tongue. It is highly recommended."

We all winced politely, except for Lewis, who awakened just at that moment.

"Yeah, that sounds pretty good," he said with a thick-tongued accent, "but what I really had my heart set on was some nose and ears. So why don't you just bring me a cheeseburger with some of that champion sauce on it and some French fries."

A slight titter went around the table out of sheer embarrassment, but Madame Tortier never cracked a smile. I was afraid she might go to the cellar for the old family guillotine and serve up "Head of Grizzard" for her next customers.

Surprisingly enough, Lewis loved Greek food. In fact, it was in Greece that I saw him eat the only salads he ever ate. The tomatoes were bright red and the cucumbers were small and fresh from the garden; he said they reminded him of summertime at his aunt's home in middle Georgia. One day, however, he discovered that all Greek salads were not created equal.

We were having lunch with some friends on their sailboat, and our kind hostess had prepared a sumptuous seafood salad. I took one look at Lewis' face — noting the nostril flair that always appeared when he didn't like what he saw — and knew there was about to be trouble. I gave him a gentle kick under the table, which he knew meant, "Shut up and eat it."

Our friends talked proudly about the fresh ingredients in the salad, but when they came to calamari, Lewis stopped them.

"What's that?" he asked.

When they told him it was squid, he grimaced and began pushing it to the sides of his plate.

"Is there something wrong with your salad?" our friend Ruth asked.

"It's not your cooking, Ruth, I swear," he said. "But I'm just not crazy about eating nothin' with its head and eyes still on. Much less something that's still wearing its shoes!"

"Lewis," I shrieked. "If you'll just try it and not think about it, I'm sure you'll like it."

"Kitty, it's not that simple. I saw *Twenty Thousand Leagues Under the Sea* twice, and I'm not about to try eating something that Kirk Douglas couldn't kill!"

After my many travels with Lewis, it finally occurred to me that I should try to capitalize on my experiences by getting him featured in an American Express ad. He could be pictured standing in front of an airplane, smiling, and I could be boarding the plane saying, "Lewis Grizzard. Best leave home without him."

The Phobia Of Grizzobia

There is a universal aspect about men that I find most puzzling — they like being sick. They don't necessarily like *getting* sick, but once there, they're perfectly content to remain in their helpless state and harvest sympathy from those forced to be around them.

Most men think the slightest wave of nausea or flash of low-grade fever is reason to hit the sheets and lie there in a commando position. "Now hear this! Now hear this!" they want to say. "Everyone within the sound of my voice is to report to the master bedroom at once, bringing extra blankets, crushed ice, fuzzy slippers, and soup of the day."

I learned at a very early age about men being sick by observing my dad. Whenever he got sick, my mother tried to leave town, but he usually caught her. She would hear the "call of the wild" from the bedroom and be forced to appear bedside to get her instructions for that particular sick day.

Once when Dad was home with a sore throat and a cold, he somehow mustered the energy to spend a couple of hours in the kitchen making pastries from scratch . . . petit fours, napoleons, and eclairs. Then he started on the main course — rolled leg of lamb — which was to be the rest of his lunch. He subscribed to the philosophy of "starve a fever and stuff a cold."

As usually was the case, the kitchen resembled the site of a demolition derby before Mom finally banished the galloping gourmet back to his sickbed. He was told to stay there and rest and not to call her again. Her white slavery days had come to an end, she said as she locked the bedroom door behind her.

This may sound like a harsh rebuke, but my dad was famous for getting sick and eating his way back to the land of the living — at Mom's expense.

Fortunately for Dad, he had just taken up a new hobby, one that proved to be a great source of entertainment while he was imprisoned in his sickroom — painting. So he painted for a couple of hours before he was suddenly hit with a new hunger attack. He knew better than to call Mother, so he carefully painted a lovely still life of a bowl of ice cream, complete with a cherry on top, and slid it under his door and out into the hallway. Then he lay down and waited for someone to come by and fill his order.

As luck would have it, my mother was the only one to pass by, and when she saw the room service request, I guess it was the cheese straw that broke the camel's back. Despite being a very kind Christian woman, she told my dad to put his artwork where the sun never shines, and then she shoved it back under the door.

The next picture Dad slid out bore a striking resemblance to Dorian Gray in his later years, and it was labeled "Mama."

Thus began my education of the male and his maladies. It was good training, of course, but it turned out to be only a primer course. When I married Lewis Grizzard, the undisputed king of sick, I discovered new dimensions of hypochondria.

We had not been married a month when Lewis came down with some dread disease that gave him a high fever and diarrhea. An intelligent person would have let their spouse call and make a doctor's appointment so they could get on the road to recovery. But not Lewis. He lay in bed until he was beginning to develop bed sores, and the only exercise he got was making his trek back and forth to the bathroom.

Finally one of his tennis partners suggested that he was getting so weak he might miss the season's opening matches if he didn't go to the doctor and get some medicine. (Note that I had made the same suggestion, but being a woman as well as a moronic wife, my advice was cast aside as silly female drivel.)

So on the recommendation of his pal, I called a well-known doctor and told the nurse his tale of woe. She said they were pretty full and couldn't see him for several days, but I told her it was an emergency — my husband couldn't write his column and I couldn't afford much more Kaopectate. That did the trick, and she gave us an appointment for early the next day.

Before I could load Lewis into the car, I had to go by my grandmother's nursing home nearby and borrow her aluminum "starting gate" so that he could put all the weight of his wasted body on it as he shuffled from the bedroom to the garage. By the time we reached the doctor's office, I needed a body bag, because Lewis had totally atrophied and was like liquid mercury on the front seat.

I leaned him on the walker again, helped him hold on, and together we finally made it into the doctor's office. The doctor saw him right away and said he thought Lewis had food poisoning, but that he would need a stool specimen to be sure of the particular strain. He delicately tried to explain the best way to obtain one and then told us to bring it back the next day.

I let it be known on the get-go that I was not helping in this medical endeavor. Lewis was on his own, but I would be glad to supply him with the required toothpick and small glass jar. I stayed as far away from the test site as I could.

The next day we took the jar, wrapped in a brown paper sack, back to the doctor, and after testing the contents he told us that Lewis had salmonella poi-

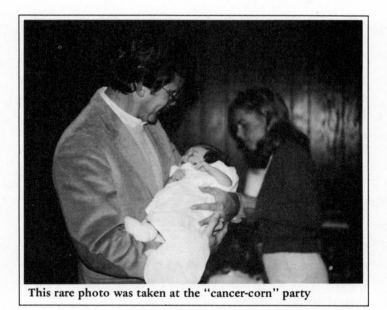

This rare photo was taken at the "cancer-corn" party

soning . . . most likely from tainted pork. He asked if we could remember eating anything like that, and Lewis said no. However, I suddenly remembered an incident earlier in the week which probably accounted for "Porky's" demise.

I had come home to find Lewis' car in the driveway with the door open, and Barney the basset standing in the back seat eating something out of a bag. I threw Barn out and picked up what I thought was a bag of garbage only to find that it contained two cartons of warm barbecue.

I found Lewis and asked him where it came from, and he said he had had it for lunch the day before and was just keeping it back there to snack on from time to time. It didn't take Dick Tracy to figure out where the bad pork had come from. All of a sudden I was worried about Barney.

The doctor gave Lewis some medicine and a lecture about day-old barbecue, and we headed home to check on the dog. I was relieved to find Barn lying in the driveway sunning himself and chewing on one of Lewis' tennis racquets.

Lewis began to recover quickly and, knowing that he was not going to die, he started enjoying the illness that made him the center of attention.

That was my first, but certainly not my last, encounter with "Grizzobia," which is the fear and ultimate contraction of every known disease in existence. And the victim doesn't even have to be exposed to become ill.

Lewis was the eternal pessimist about his health, and all of his friends knew about Grizzobia. After his bout with food poisoning and the resultant weight loss, they would torture him with statements like, "Gollllly, Lewis, you're so skinny. Did you drive here?" He would come home and lie prostrate on the sofa for hours because they had called him "chicken breast" and "the ninety-eight-pound weakling poster boy."

I would try to cajole him out of his bad mood by telling him that they were just a bunch of pudgies who were jealous of his slim physique. But that was the wrong thing to say. They had also told him not to stand too close to the Slim Jim canisters in the 7-11 stores because someone might mistake him for one.

It was useless — he was convinced that he had an incurable illness and was wasting away to nothing. (Some of my friends insisted he was already nothing, regardless of his size.)

Lewis never got just a cold; it was always the flu. He could even tell you what strain, if you were stupid enough to ask, and it usually was whatever the Centers for Disease Control had decided was in vogue that flu season.

The year of the Legionnaires' disease scare, for instance, Lewis was convinced he had the only undiagnosed case in the country. He contracted it while giving a speech at a Shriners' convention. Early in the program he broke out with a violent sneezing fit, which resulted in a runny nose, sore throat, and earache. He heroically finished his speech and staggered back to his room to recuperate.

The hotel did not have a bar, nor was there one nearby, but Lewis was convinced he would die without some alcohol to kill the germ. He finally called the front desk of the motel and promised a young bellboy, Luther, that he would pay for his entire Vo-Tech education if Luther would find some spirits to put him out of his misery. Luther returned about an hour later triumphantly carrying his purchase, which he got from his uncle's all-night gas station. It was a full bottle of Deuce Juice, which he assured Lewis was a uniquely blended "wine" that would relieve his symptoms.

Lewis paid Luther handsomely and quickly downed a plastic glass full of the "juice." It fixed him up, all right. He had stomach pains so bad he forgot about Legionnaires' disease and re-diagnosed himself as having bleeding ulcers. By the next morning it had been upgraded to stomach cancer.

Another night we were watching a television show starring Karl Malden. He was a steel worker in Pittsburgh, and he had a stroke early in the program. The story showed the anguish he went through as he tried to continue to raise his family and work with his partial paralysis.

By the time the program ended, Lewis' speech had become slurred, his left side had gone numb, and he dragged his left foot uselessly all the way back to the bedroom.

Several weeks later he was invited to speak to a bunch of fertilizer salesmen at a beautiful ocean resort. We went for a walk on the beach that afternoon and kicked our way through the shallow surf. Suddenly Lewis fell to his knees, moaning and grabbing his foot. I was sure he had either been stung by a jellyfish, shocked by an electric eel, or, worse, struck by a tiny sand shark.

As I knelt to inspect what I was sure would be a grotesque wound, "Flipper" rolled around in the shallow waves, writhing in pain. I couldn't find any visible injury, so I asked him to point it out. A half-hidden, partially broken sand dollar was the culprit that had inflicted a slight cut.

He limped back to the motel room, using me as a human crutch, and I administered first aid. I poured Listerine on the area in question and then had him gargle in case of spreading infectious halitosis.

I completely forgot about Lewis' injury until that night at dinner when the head manure man told a joke and mentioned foot and mouth disease. Quicker than you could say "animal husbandry," Lewis was pulling up his pants leg under the head table and looking for any telltale signs of infection. He had failed to make the connection between livestock and the disease, but it was inconsequential at that point. He was convinced he had contracted hoof and mouth. I told him he was merely suffering from "shell shock."

DID YOU SAY CAPRICORN
OR CANCER-CORN?

Perhaps the most horrifying hypochondriac manifestation that Lewis ever pulled on me was the malignancy he found in his mouth one day. We had been to a Christmas party at a friend's house and had eaten lots of goodies while the kids were entertained by Santa Claus. We had to leave early to drop off a column at Lewis' office before we went home.

As we were driving down the interstate, he turned to me, looked in the rear view mirror at the same time, and said, "Kitty, I have something very sad to tell you. It's going to break you up."

He had taken his hands off the wheel and was pulling his lips apart to expose his gums, all the while making these disgusting sucking noises and scratching a large freckle on his arm. I grabbed the wheel, since he didn't seem to be interested in it, and asked him what was wrong.

"I have found a large immovable bump on my gum next to a tooth," he said, "and there's no doubt in my mind that it's cancer of the gum." As additional confirmation of the disease, he had noticed that the big red freckle on his arm had somehow reproduced and now there was a little brown one beside it.

Trying to keep my composure, I listened as he recited the "Seven Early Warning Signs of Cancer." These he had memorized perfectly, and they were practically his daily mantra. He had copies pasted on the sun visors in all his cars, on the backs of all his tapes, in his travel shaving kit, on the bathroom mirror, and even taped to the side of his typewriter.

He started telling me the type of disfiguring surgery that would be necessary to remove the malignant tumor, all the while still making those disgusting sucking noises. Suddenly he said, "Hey! Look at this!" He stuck his finger in his mouth and pulled out a popcorn kernel that had been wedged between his tooth and gum. I remembered that he had eaten almost an entire bowl of Pop Goes the Corn while standing in line to see Santa. (He had gotten a hot tip from our host that behind Santa's beard loomed the lovely face of a college coed who baby-sat for the family on occasion. She was the only St. Nick they could find on short notice, and unfortunately Lewis had once seen her in a bikini.)

As far as the change in his freckle went, that was another story in itself. The little brown speck beside the old red freckle was nothing more than a spot of tobacco stuck to his arm.

He was partially right about the mole, however; there had been a change. I had been watching this unusual spot for months and had finally realized that it was, indeed, special. In the tradition of the "mood ring," Lewis was the possessor of a "mood mole." When he was nervous or scared, it itched. When he was happy, it turned a pale pink. Jealousy or anger turned it purple, and when he had too much to drink, it virtually disappeared by blending in with his other freckles.

I could always tell when he was getting ready to lose his temper because his MM would shine like a neon beacon and begin to pulsate, the way a vein in the forehead acts on some people.

To add even more mystery, beside the "mood mole" was a "weather freckle." When the weather was going to turn cold, the WF would get premature goose pimples all around it; when it was windy, the single hair in it would blow furiously; when there was rain, it was wet; and a sunny day brought on a crisp, red finish to it. This usually occurred on the beach where Lewis was always mad and always hot.

He was always mad because there were always very athletic, deeply tanned young men playing frisbee, and all the ladies on the beach loved to watch them leap and grab the disc, exposing all their muscles . . . when they could have been listening to him tell stories. Lewis would mutter under his umbrella about what a ridiculous game frisbee was to play in public, and his mood mole would mix with his weather freckle until the spot resembled a throbbing, lavender Easter egg.

A change in a mole, of course, is one of the seven early warning signs, so I encouraged Lewis to have it checked. But like so many other men (only in his case, worse), he was extremely reluctant to go to doctors or dentists.

One would think that if a hypochondriac enjoyed the attention he got by being sick, then that same person should relish the attention paid to him by doctors, nurses, receptionists, and even their parking lot attendants. But not so. Why? Simple — men are cowards when it comes to any sort of pain.

When I was little, I used to watch those cowboy movies where the good guy would get shot, and one of his pals would have to dig the bullet out with the nearest piece of barbed wire or broken glass. The wounded dude would lie there and grimace like he was on the way out, but he'd make a remarkable recovery right there on the range without so much as a Bayer. Consequently, I grew up believing that *all* men could endure tortures of the damned when it came to pain and injury. Such a fool was I.

Not only can they not stand pain, they can't watch anyone else in pain either. When my sister Helen was having her first baby, husband Rocky promised to stay with her in the delivery room. He did fine as long as his only job was mopping her brow throughout a long labor, but when the big moment came and the doctor told him to watch in the mirror, he went out like a light. A couple of orderlies grabbed a piece of the Rock and dragged him to Helen's recovery room.

When he came to and I told him he had a healthy son, he wanted to see him. I escorted Rocky to the nursery, explaining that since the baby was premature he would be an unusual color. He naively asked what color, and I took pleasure in answering, "Yellow . . . like his dad."

Women, of course, not only have to endure the real pain of childbirth — and the humiliation of having our legs spread open like a chicken wing while what seems like the whole Moose Lodge is looking on — but years later we also have to suffer through menopause. And not a mental menopause like men; ours is a sweat-when-it's-freezing, shiver-when-it's-stifling physical menopause. Meanwhile, our men say such condescending niceties as, "Don't mind her, she's going through the change."

And what about the elective pain we may endure to endear ourselves to our men — face lifts, tummy tucks, eyelid lifts, and BBT (bigger bosoms by tomorrow)? Do they ever experience anything like that?

Just mention the phrase "bend over" in a crowd of men at a cocktail party and watch their saddlebags start to quiver.

When Lewis had a blood study done in conjunction with his bout with food poisoning, another interesting diagnosis was made: He had low blood sugar. Following a glucose tolerance test, it was determined that he had hypoglycemia.

He was elated. The more he learned about the symptoms, the more excited he got. He now had a legitimate reason to shake when he was hungry, bark at those around him with no provocation, and have loss in energy in the afternoons. I wasn't very sympathetic, because I suffered the same symptoms every time I went on the Ayds Reducing Plan.

But his was different, he said. He reveled in comparing symptoms with fellow sufferers, and he enjoyed "customizing" his new restricted diet. Suddenly I knew nothing about nutrition and he was the expert.

"Kitty, I bet you didn't know that fruit has sugar in it, did you?"

"Of course I did, the same kind of sugar that's in this tomato I'd like to smash in your hypoglycemic, overly fructosed yapper."

Then he would proceed to down a few beers, followed by several vodka tonics, and complain the next morning about the imbalance in his blood sugar. "You must be feeding me the wrong things," he would surmise.

I finally bought him a bottle of Geritol. "Your blood isn't too sweet," I said, "just tired. And so am I . . . of hearing about it."

Lewis' physical and mental health fetishes were so strong that one day it occurred to me he could benefit from a psychiatrist. He needed someone to act as a sounding board and to provide an impartial ear to the pressures of being a public figure. This was the most idiotic thing he'd ever heard of, he said, until one day a tennis buddy suggested the same thing. Then it was brilliant.

I knew a number of qualified people in the counseling field who could have provided excellent help, but he preferred to follow the lead of his tennis chums and visit Dr. Paul Parrot.

I waited enthusiastically on the afternoon of Lewis' first appointment. When he arrived home, I asked how it went. Great, he said; he had finally found someone who could listen objectively to his problems. I was delighted and asked if he could share any of their conversation with me.

"Sure, I'll give you a good example," he said. "I told Dr. Parrot I have a problem with women. I always seem to make them mad when I don't really mean to. But they just don't have the mental capacity to grasp how demanding my job is . . . being a star and all."

And what was the doctor's response? "What I hear you saying, Lewis, is that you are a very misunderstood individual. Is that correct?"

Give the man a cigar. He figured it out.

Lewis was really impressed by Dr. Parrot's insight, and he said they talked non-stop for nearly an hour. The doctor agreed with almost everything he said (at $125 an hour, Lewis could have said he was a chicken and Dr. Parrot would have provided Purina poultry snacks), which made Lewis feel much better. He couldn't wait for his next appointment.

In the months that followed, I took great interest in asking Lewis what he and the doctor discussed at each session. Apparently the doctor's comments were almost always the same: "Lewis, I hear what you're saying. . . ." or, "Now, let me ask you this — What do *you* think about that?" And Lewis would lay open his "misunderstood" heart.

Just once I wanted to meet with Dr. Parrot and say, "Are you nuts?" But I had to remember that it was my idea. I do have a plan for getting back, however. I intend to write a layperson's book on self-analysis entitled, *Irresponsible and Proud of It!* There's no doubt that I'm as qualified to analyze the neurotic mind as Lewis' Dr. Parrot.

SHE WHO LAUGHS LAST LAUGHS HARDEST

Much has been written about Lewis' problems with his heart, and I would not want to minimize the severity of his condition. Nonetheless, the circumstances surrounding the original diagnosis are worth revealing.

I discussed Lewis' insomnia in an earlier chapter, but another reason he couldn't get to sleep some nights was the pounding pulse in his neck. I suggested several times that he see a doctor about it, but he ignored me. Then when one of his tennis opponents finally complained that the pulsating vein was distracting him at the net, Lewis finally gave in and went to the doctor.

He had been told years before that he had a congenital value problem and that someday it would have to be fixed. That someday had arrived, the doctor told him.

Lewis, of course, blamed his condition on me because I was the one who constantly brought up words like "check-up" and "examination."

The idea of open-heart surgery scared him plenty, but on one of our preoperative meetings with the surgeon, I discovered something that scared him even more — catheterization. (For the uninitiated, that's the tube inserted through the you-know-what to drain the bladder.) The doctor tried to calm him, saying that although he would be catheterized, he would be so heavily sedated he'd never know it. But the doctor might as well have been talking to the wall, because Lewis just sat comatose staring out the window.

When we got to the car, he blew up and said he was not going to have the operation, no way, forget it, N - O!

"Why not? You know how important it is," I said.

"I don't care. I saw a friend once with a catheter, and I'm not going to have any yellow pocketbook hanging from my bed!"

I tried to reason with him, but the more I said, the more he yelled. Then I made the mistake of telling him that I had had a catheter with my last baby and it didn't hurt a bit.

"I don't care if you had one at the fifty-yard line during half time of the Georgia-Georgia Tech game. I'm not having one, and that's final!" he screamed.

The last thing he said to me before going under the anesthetic the morning of his surgery was, "I'm holding you personally responsible for any catheters found in or around my body."

It should go without saying that Lewis was not exactly the most pleasant patient the hospital had ever had. He hollered and fussed and moaned and groaned and demanded to be released from the moment they pulled the tube out of his throat. At times I wanted to reinsert it. When he got out of intensive care, he was ready to go home, but he was destined to spend another week harassing the staff and barking orders to me about his care.

For several days he was convinced that the surgery had *not* been a success and that he was actually living in a dream. I agreed . . . a nightmare.

One day two nurses, who bore an amazing resemblance to Roosevelt Grier and Dick Butkus, came into Lewis' room and asked me to leave for a moment. As I walked out of the room, I heard one of them say the words that would give me solace for years, words that would cloak me in comfort and soothe my wounded pride during our divorce, words that convinced me that God really is a registered nurse in starched white clothes and soft rubber-soled shoes.

One of the nurses said, "Now, Mr. Grizzard, Nurse Quattlebaum and I are going to turn you over to adjust your catheter. It seems to be leaking."

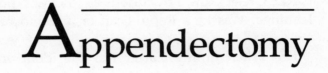Appendectomy

I was recently interviewed by the nationally acclaimed magazine *Rural Detective*, which is noted for its use of flagrant yellow journalism. As I was questioned about Lewis and our life together, it occurred to me that perhaps a copy of that very sensitive interview might be an appropriate note to end on.

RD: Well, Kitty . . .

KS: It's Mrs. Schmook to you.

RD: Excuse me, Mrs. Schmuck.

KS: Just call me Kitty.

RD: Great. Now, I'm curious as to Lewis' political leanings. Was he a Republican or a Democrat?

KS: When Jimmy Carter was President and invited him to the White House, he was a staunch Democrat. But when the Carters lost their lease and their clout, Lewis hired an accountant and became a dedicated Republican. He now has a small plastic statue of Ronald Reagan on the dash of his Mercedes 380SL.

RD: Who was Lewis' favorite President?

KS: Whose picture is on a one hundred dollar bill?

RD: Let's move on to music. What sort did Lewis listen to most?

KS: Anyone who knows him knows that he adores country music.

RD: No pop or classics?

KS: You must be crazy. Are you sure you don't write for *Psycho Today?* The only "pop" he liked was a cold one after tennis. And the classics? He may have had a slight interest in Boots Randolph's "Classical Sax," but that's about it.

RD: Not much cultural interest where music was concerned, huh?

KS: Look, I'm trying to tell you, the only culture around our house was in the buttermilk he poured over his cornbread. In fact, and maybe this will end this subject, I tried introducing Lewis to opera once while we were married. It would have been easier taking Moshe Dayan's eye patch away from him. Lewis thought Pavorotti was an Italian meat sauce and Placido Domingo was a birth defect.

He accompanied me under great duress. I chose Bizet's *Carmen*, thinking it would be a hearty, masculine story with enough action to keep him interested. After the first fifteen minutes, he woke up and claimed he was sick. He said he'd go outside, get some air, and be back at "half time."

Three hours later when the opera ended, I was looking around the lobby for him. I spotted him and as he approached, I could smell a pungent odor from fifty feet away. He smelled like the grand prize winner of the Vidalia onion "Eat'um Up" contest, and he had a telltale sign of mustard on his shirt.

"Where have you been?" I asked disgustedly. "I thought you were sick!"

"I am. I've been walking around outside getting some air," he said innocently.

"Oh, and that's why you look and smell like an onion-ated tube steak?"

"I did walk up to the Varsity for a snack, and now I'm back to pick up my lovely bride and take her home." With that he let out a series of burps that made his eyes water and his nostrils the size of basketball hoops. He stopped belching long enough to add, "How was the rest of the show? Was it over when the fat lady sang?" He broke himself up with that crack.

"Lewis, not only are you a liar," I said, "but you are obviously content with being an unpolished dolt the rest of your life. I have tried to broaden your scope by introducing you to yet another spectrum of the music world, and all you can do is sleep, drool, and eat. I give up! No more symphony, no more concerts in the park, and certainly no more opera!"

"Look, Kitty, I'm sorry. But how can you expect me to enjoy some show where all the women look like Kate Smith and sound like a pack of dogs chasing a gutwagon? Plus, you can't smoke or drink in your chair, they don't sell popcorn, and them little binoculars you have don't fit on my glasses, so I can't see nothin' anyways."

"Just forget it," I said. "Remain an artistic ignoramus all your life. I hope you're broke one day and have to take a job as an art or music critic!"

Now does that answer your question?

RD: Yes, that thoroughly covers it. How about musical instruments. Did Lewis play any?

KS: Yes, the cassette player in his old Cadillac. He couldn't work the one in his new Mercedes. He also played his zipper.

RD: Oh, the zither. That's interesting.

KS: No, I said *zipper!* He played hambone on his body and ended up by running his thumbnail up his zipper for the big finale.

RD: How fascinating. Tell me, I'm sure Lewis read a lot. Who were his favorite writers?

KS: Hugh Hefner, Ludlow Porch, and William F. Buckley. He had more of Buckley's books on his shelf than anyone else's because he felt it raised his intellectual level just having them around. In actuality, he never read one because he never understood even the chapter titles. He also kept getting him mixed up with Gore Vidal. He was always terrified of ending up on a talk show with Buckley and having to talk to him.

RD: What was Lewis' greatest fear?

KS: He had two, really. One was being trapped in a hot tub with Jerry Falwell and Prince, and the other was that one of his ex-wives might write a book about him one day.

RD: I understand you have. Why did you?

KS: Well, let's just say that it looked to me like Lewis needed some new material, so I gave him a little something to yap about. I'm also tired of being the butt of all his divorce jokes. It's time to hear from the other side, I'd say.

RD: How about when you were alone at night. What did Lewis like to do?

KS: Have insomnia and watch reruns of "Divorce Court." He used to place bets on who the judge would find for.

RD: How about things that bugged him. What was his pet peeve?

KS: Next to women, I'd say television evangelists. They used to write him letters and ask if he knew whether or not he was going to heaven. Then they'd go on about how "the heathen doth rage." In the same letter they'd tell him that it had been called to their attention that he needed to be prayed for, and that he had been placed in their "Little Lost Lamb File." However, the actual praying could not commence till he had sent in a minimum of fifty dollars. For five hundred dollars, he got prayed up to the bottom rung of Jacob's Ladder, and for a thousand, he was assured of a front-row seat in the engine of the Glory Train when it left for heaven. I told Lewis not to send them a dime . . . I was praying for him a lot harder than they were, and I was free.

RD: Did he believe in God?

KS: Yes, twice. Once when he escaped from Chicago to come back and write for the Atlanta newspapers, and when Georgia beat Notre Dame for the national collegiate football championship.

RD: Did he ever go to church?

KS: He went a few times at my request but then he said it was just too boring. He wasn't used to having to listen to someone else talk for an hour, and they never asked him to come up and tell any of *his* stories. It also made him mad that they wouldn't let him smoke in the pew.

RD: Lewis is always making fun of Yankees, and he says it is a "Yankee trait" to put ketchup on scrambled eggs. What was his favorite condiment?

KS: Trojans.

RD: Hmmm . . . moving right along, what type of movie does Lewis like best?

KS: He likes sort of a combination soft porn and martial arts . . . those karate kind.

RD: Did he have a favorite film?

KS: Yeah, he loved *The Gland Hotel*. He liked all the hand to gland contact in it.

RD: I know Lewis plays a lot of tennis. How was his forehand?

KS: Bigger than his forearm.

RD: Are you saying that Lewis did not have a muscular build?

KS: Have you ever seen the legs on a Chihuahua?

RD: Would you consider Lewis a gourmet?

KS: Why, yes. He often ate a seven-course meal. That consisted of a six-pack and a bologna sandwich.

RD: Well, was he handy around the house?

KS: Are you kidding? After we were divorced, it took twelve people to change a light bulb in his house — one ex-wife to tell him it was out, one person to take notes so he could write about it later, one electrician, one accountant to pay the electrician, one lawyer to file suit against the Five-Year Light Bulb Company, one investment banker to buy the Five-Year Light Bulb Company, and six of his fans to watch while he did his Reddy Kilowatt imitation for them.

RD: Is it true that Lewis had bulldogs on his underwear?

KS: No, but they could bark after a few days.

RD: What turns Lewis on?

KS: I don't know, but if you find out, I wish you'd let me know. I think the secret to that lies in the vault with the Coke formula.

RD: In all seriousness, was Lewis hard to live with? Was he moody?

KS: Did Golda wear sandals?

RD: Was there ever any one thing you did personally that really made him mad?

KS: Putting almonds in the green beans was never popular.

RD: Do you think Lewis will ever stop remarrying?

KS: Yes, when he has enough ex-wives for an all-girl softball team.

RD: Who would be the ideal woman for Lewis?

KS: Venus de Mama.

RD: What advice would you give the next Mrs. Grizzard?

KS: Go west, young woman, go west.

RD: Are you sorry you and Lewis are divorced? Do you worry about him?

KS: Yes, I'm sorry about the divorce, but I believe in living life not "the way we were" but the way we *are*, and we are friends. And yes, I do worry about him a lot . . . mainly about his teeth.

RD: Well, Kitty, it looks like that's about it. Anything you'd like to add?

KS: Well, just one question for you, off the record.

RD: You bet. What's that?

KS: Did you interview Lewis about me?

RD: Yes, as a matter of fact, we did.

KS: And what did he say?

RD: He said he didn't know what a Kathy Schmook was, but he guessed it was either a drink with an umbrella in it or some kind of German weenie. He said he had heard, however, that there was a crazy woman in Montana writing a book about him.